Dark Knights 4

The Dark Humor of Police Officers

The Police Academy

Robert L. Bryan

Copyright © 2019 Robert L. Bryan All rights reserved First Edition

Printed in the United States of America

For Meghan. Always in my heart!

From the Author

Thank you for purchasing DARK KNIGHTS 4. I hope you enjoyed it. This is the 4th installment in the Dark Knights series.

DARK KNIGHTS was the first in the series and followed my career in the NYC Transit Police and NYPD through a series of darkly funny stories about my experiences and the characters I met during my career.

DARK KNIGHTS 2 is a humorous account of the two years I spent as a Border Patrol Agent prior to my NYPD career.

DARK KNIGHTS 3 is the humorous continuation of my NYPD career.

You can find all of my books on Amazon – I hope you enjoy

CONTENTS

PROLOGUE 6

INTRODUCTION 9

CHAPTER 1   GENESIS OF THE POLICE ACADEMY 14

CHAPTER 2: NEW YORK CITY'S POLICE ACADEMIES 20

CHAPTER 3: GRABBING MY RUBBER BAND 41

CHAPTER 4: THE RISK TAKERS 65

CHAPTER 5: THE PANAMA LOTTERY COMES TO POLICE SCIENCE 81

CHAPTER 6: HIGHWAY 86

CHAPTER 7: YOU WANT TO STEP OUTSIDE? 91

CHAPTER 8: EVALUATIONS 100

CHAPTER 9: WORKING OUT 103

CHAPTER 10: A HAPPY VISIT 106

CHAPTER 11: THE ROTTEN APPLE 111

CHAPTER 12: MY RECRUITS 114

CHAPTER 13: ROLE PLAYS 126

CHAPTER 14: GRADUATION 138

CHAPTER 15: THE RUBBER BAND DOES ITS JOB 146

CHAPTER 16: THE WRONG REVIEW MATERIAL 168

CHAPTER 17: BREAKING AWAY 173

CHAPTER 18: THE LAST RUBBER BAND 188

EPILOGUE 194

PROLOGUE

When I was in the fifth grade at Our Lady of Fatima elementary school, in Queens, New York City, my desk was in the last row, directly adjacent to the windows. In those days, the school had no cafeteria or accommodations to care for students at lunch time, so the kids were sent home for lunch – or to roam the streets for an hour. Every day, just before lunch time and dismissal at the end of the day, I would observe the same scene outside the window. The nasty old lady crossing guard in her dirty blue uniform with white safety belt would take up her position at the intersection of 30th Avenue and 80th Street. I actually liked to see this mean old woman with the snarl on her face and the cigarette dangling from her lips because without a watch or a clock in the classroom, she was the time piece that let me know salvation was at hand.

This scene repeated itself day after day during the school year with only one occasional break in the routine. Every now and then, the miserable old lady was replaced by a smiling policeman. Unlike the old woman, the policeman always seemed happy to be talking to the kids and parents while he kept the students safe. I was always happy to see the crossing guard and the approaching dismissal, but I was especially happy to see the policeman.

I have always looked at police officers as being something positive. Aside from the school crossing guard, I had very little interaction with police growing up, but my parents would always tell me if I was in any trouble, I should look for a police officer to help me. That was the theme – a police officer would help me. I was not warned that a police officer might beat me, or falsely arrest me, or violate my constitutional rights. To the contrary, I grew up believing (and I still believe) that police are present to preserve my rights.

When I was 24-years old, I had just returned to New York City after spending two years on the Mexican Border as a Border Patrol Agent. I had decided several years earlier that I wanted a career in law enforcement, but I wanted to live in New York City, so I left the Border Patrol to take a job as an investigator with the New York City Inspector General's Office of the Department of Sanitation. While I investigated garbage corruption, I waited for the opportunity to become of police officer. Specifically, I was on the civil service list to be appointed to the New York City Transit Police Department.

During this period of my life I spent many nights socializing with friends at Kate Cassidy's Irish Pub, a local watering hole on Woodhaven Boulevard in Queens. Kevin was, and still is, a good friend of mine, and he possessed the type of gregarious personality that made it seem like he knew everything about everyone who entered that bar. The pub had the reputation for being a cop hang out, and Kevin knew all the cops and where they worked. I was fascinated by two groups of cops Kevin introduced me to. First, there were the members of the 112th Precinct Detective Squad, with their suits and pinky rings, chomping on fat cigars (that's right – smoking in a bar was legal at that time). They were all very affable fellows, and they had the greatest stories. One of the detectives named Louie, was actually memorialized in the Odd Couple TV series. Louie was in the Movie & TV Unit during the time the Odd Couple was filming its opening and closing scenes on location in New York City. Louie is visible in uniform in the opening and closing credits and was written into the scene by approaching Oscar (Jack Klugman) and glaring at him as Oscar peered through the window of a Times Square peep show.

As much as I liked and admired the detectives, there was another group of cops Kevin introduced me to who intrigued me even more. There were four Police Academy instructors who were regulars at the pub. These men just seemed so calm and cool in everything they did and said. They seemed to have all the answers – and why not? These police officers were the role models who were shaping the minds and bodies of new recruits. They had to be the best – the cream of the crop. I could only imagine the rigorous standards that must be in place for a police officer to qualify as an instructor. The idea of one day being a detective appealed to me, but the thought of ever being one of those elite academy instructors did not seem like reality.

Remember, at one time I did believe in Santa Claus too.

INTRODUCTION

The platform at the late hour looked like something post-apocalyptic. There was no one there except for me and my silent partner. I stared into the black tunnel, willing those red lights to blink back at me, so at least I would have interaction with something. The quiet was chilling. I was a product of the times when New York City's nickname had sardonically transitioned from Fun City to Fear City, so I had been programmed to believe that nothing good happened in a deserted subway station. I held my hand out to feel for the movement of air that comes as the train pushes it along, but there was nothing. Nothing but the dirty grey concrete floor and the worn yellow stripe of paint along the platform edge under my shoes. It occurred to me that I shouldn't be anywhere near that yellow stripe, but who was going to knock me off the platform – my partner?

During my limited experience on the subway system, I never found any similarities in the words *subway* and *quiet*. My sampling of the subway environment was almost always during the daytime when the trains and stations were a seething mass of humanity. Everyone from every walk of life was shoulder to shoulder, in each other's faces, no personal space, no exceptions. The only times I rode late night trains was coming from Madison Square Garden after a Rangers game or Yankee Stadium after a ball game, when the trains were filled with happy or unhappy fans, depending on the result of the game. The concept of a subway station being so quiet that echoes were audible was foreign to me.

It was 1:00 AM and my partner had said nothing more than "follow me," when we turned out after roll call. Fourteen hours earlier, I stood proudly in full dress uniform at Brooklyn College with the rest of my classmates as we graduated from the Police Academy. During the previous six months I had grown comfortable wrapped in the security blanket of the academy. During training, my biggest problems were dealing with the horrific conditions, or possibly getting yelled at in class. Everything became a routine. I woke up in the morning, showered, dressed and rode the bus and subway to upper Manhattan. Sitting in class, my biggest decision was usually where to go for lunch. Would I face the stress of time pressure in taking the train one stop to the Bronx to dine at one of the many restaurants near Yankee Stadium, or would I get my sustenance from the truck parked daily in front of the academy, known affectionately as Perry's Dirty Water Dogs. Then came graduation, and in the blink of an eye, I transitioned from the world of speeches, photos, and well wishes, to standing on the deserted platform of the Parsons Boulevard underground subway station in the Jamaica section of Queens. Instead of optimistic words from the Chief of the Transit Police Department I was now receiving silence from a twenty plus year veteran officer who wanted nothing to do with dragging around a rookie fresh out of the academy all night.

At approximately 1:15AM the veteran turned to me and cleared his throat. This was it. This was going to be my Dali Lama moment when words of wisdom would be spoken that would profoundly impact the rest of my life.

"Kid – the best thing you can do is forget all that crap they taught you at the Police Academy."

"What?" I was confused. Why would I do that? Hadn't the instructors spent the last six months drilling me with police science, law, social science, firearms training, and physical tactics? Hadn't they transitioned me from a civilian into a well-trained professional police officer? Why would I want to forget about the Police Academy?

Fast forward five years. What a way to start. I was assigned to a classroom in the basement. I didn't even know the Police Academy had classrooms in the basement, but there I was, a brand-new instructor walking the halls in the bowels of the building trying to find my recruit company.

A few days earlier, it had all seemed like so much fun and excitement. One day, I was patrolling subway stations for the New York City Transit Police and the next day I was detailed to the New York City Police Academy as an instructor. It had been easy to get all hyped up in the group of new instructors completing the two-week Methods of Instruction course, egging each other on, gaining some degree of comfort speaking in front of a group.

As I turned the corner in the basement hall, the irony was not lost on me. I was a transit cop, and my beat as an academy instructor was still underground. Off in the distance I saw a male in the light blue recruit shirt and uniform tie standing in front of the classroom door at the military position of parade rest. This was the company sergeant on the lookout for the instructor. My nervousness bothered me. I was a police officer – I was not allowed to be afraid – to show the tenseness that was growing in my head and heart. I was supposed to be a warrior and protector, preferably wrapped up with comedian to ease the fears of others. I was not supposed to feel this nervous about entering a classroom of police recruits for the first time.

I was close enough to the classroom that I could hear the company sergeant warn the company to stand by. I was desperately trying to hide how fearful I was, and I hoped the perspiration I could not control was not visibly staining my uniform shirt.

"Hey Bobby." The call stopped me five steps from the classroom door. Al Benson held his arms out to the side. "Where are you going? This is my room."

I pulled the daily schedule from my pocket and pointed to Company 7. "See, Al, I'm in Basement 05."

Al shook his finger. "That's not the basement – it's the sub-basement"

"Sub-basement," I exclaimed. "You mean there's something lower than the basement?"

My initial reaction when I emerged from the sub-basement stairwell was that I was the subject of some type of hazing. The hall was dimly lit and quiet. I passed the print shop and the janitor's quarters, and several storage rooms. I turned and was headed back to the stairway when I was startled by a voice from behind me. "Sir, I think you're looking for us."

It was the company sergeant who had taken the initiative to abandon his post at the door of the classroom at the desolate, dark end of the sub-basement to initiate a search mission for his lost instructor. I could safely say without any doubt, my career as an academy instructor truly started at the bottom. The same could also be said for police academy training in general.

CHAPTER 1   GENESIS OF THE POLICE ACADEMY

Professional, well-trained police are a relatively new phenomenon. During the early history of policing, individual citizens were largely responsible for maintaining law and order among themselves. Those who served as constables and justices of the peace did so voluntarily and were not typically paid for their services. Shire reeves, or sheriffs, were employed full-time to oversee law enforcement activities within their shires in England and their counties in the colonies. Through the centuries, those practices played a significant role in the history of policing around the world.

The loosely based system of social control worked quite well for centuries, particularly in more rural and less populated regions. However, the late 1700s and early 1800s saw a population explosion in major cities in the United States and England. Riots and civil unrest were common, and it became increasingly clear that there was a need for a more permanent and professional form of law enforcement that would carry the official authority of the government.

Perhaps the most powerful advocate for a professional, well trained police force was Sir Robert Peel, a Minister of Parliament who served as Home Secretary for the United Kingdom in the 1820s. In 1829, Peel established the Metropolitan Police Services in London. With the founding of London's police force, Peel became widely regarded by criminologists and historians alike as the father of modern policing. British police officers are still known affectionately as "Bobbies" in honor of his first name, Robert.

The concept of a centralized, professional police force was a tough sell initially and was met with a tremendous amount of resistance. The public feared that a police force would essentially behave as another arm of the military. As a result, there was an understandable reluctance to agree to be controlled by what many assumed would be an occupying force. To overcome this opposition, Peel is known for laying the framework for what a police force should be comprised of and how a good police officer should conduct himself. While there is debate as to whether he ever clearly enumerated his ideas in any sort of list format, it is generally agreed that he created what are to this day considered to be the primary principles of policing.

Peel's efforts were very effective in assuaging public fears and concerns. In addition to the principles of policing, Peel and his supporters took other measures to ensure that there was a clear distinction between professional police officers and the military. Police wore blue uniforms in contrast to the bright red of the royal armed forces. They were forbidden to carry guns, and at all times the importance of maintaining the public trust was impressed upon members of the force. As much as he advanced the concept of modern policing, the police in Peel's era were light years away from the professionally trained officers of today. Consider, for example, a recruiting poster for Peel's police circa 1839.

- Your working hours will be eight, ten, or twelve-hour shifts, seven days a week. Every encouragement will be given to officers to grow beards as shaving is regarded as unhealthy. However, beards must not exceed two inches in length.

- Uniform will be worn all the time, to prevent accusations of spying on the public, whilst in ordinary clothes. A duty band will be worn to indicate whether you are on duty or not.

- You are NOT allowed to vote in elections.

- You must not gossip with the public. In particular, avoid conversations with female servants or other women on duty. Do not walk or converse with your comrades, merely exchange a word and pass on.

- You will walk about 20 miles per shift.

- No rest days are allowed and only one week holiday per annum, unpaid.

- No meal breaks are allowed. The top hat may be used to hold a snack. You must inform the Superintendent before you associate, eat, or drink with any civilians.

- Before attending for medical examination and interview to join the police, it is advisable to have a bath.

- You are NOT allowed the sit down in any public houses at any time.

- You must expect a hostile reception from all sections of the public and be prepared to be assaulted, stoned or stabbed in the course of your duties.

Being a police officer in Peel's era sounded like a really great job, didn't it?

This concept of the modern police force soon found its way to the United States, though it was not implemented in exactly the same manner as it was in London. Due to the extreme political influence during the 19th century, there were virtually no standards for hiring or training police officers. Essentially, politicians within each ward would hire men that would agree to help them stay in office and not consider whether they were the most qualified people for the job. Police officials were appointed through political affiliations and because of this they were frequently unintelligent and untrained. New policemen heard a brief speech from a high-ranking officer, received a hickory club, a whistle, and a key to the callbox, and were sent out on the street to work with an experienced officer. Not only were the policemen untrained in law, but they operated within a criminal justice system that generally placed little emphasis upon legal procedure.

During the period, American police forces were notorious for their corruption and promotion of the "third degree," or torture methods in interrogation. Alexander S. "Clubber" Williams, a corrupt cop in New York's Vice District symbolized the era when he told a reporter that "there is more law in the end of a nightstick than in the decision of the Supreme Court."

During the latter stages of the 19th century there were very few initiatives in police training. During this era, however, increasing attention was directed to professionalism and training as a result of the public's growing contempt of political corruption and social disorder. For example, in 1877, the Cincinnati Police Department, and in 1903 the Cleveland Police Department established training programs for police recruits where on a weekly basis captains conducted classes that covered state laws, city ordinances and department regulations. It was not until 1907, however, that August Vollmer, Marshall of the city of Berkeley, California, set forth the idea for the first formal police academy. He was convinced that the principle problems with all police departments was directly related to lack of training, and in 1908 he developed a police school which covered a wide variety of subjects such as police methods and procedures, fingerprinting, first aid, and criminal law.

CHAPTER 2: NEW YORK CITY'S POLICE ACADEMIES

Following Vollmer's lead, in 1909 the New York City Police Department opened its first police academy which provided recruits with training in firearms, departmental rules and regulations, police procedures and criminal law. But it was Theodore Roosevelt, more than a decade earlier who sowed the seeds for New York City's first Police Academy

In 1895 Roosevelt — fearless and righteous and full of zeal — was appointed New York City Police Commissioner and was assigned to clean up the Big Apple at what many said was its dirtiest, most rotten moment in history.

In the 1890s, New York City was a bustling chaotic city with no traffic lights and few traffic rules; horse carriages zigzagged any way up and down any street and a small cadre of two dozen tall "Broadway Squad" officers helped pedestrians to cross the major intersections. Four elevated train lines striped the island, spewing coal dust and granting passengers voyeuristic glimpses into second floor windows. Top-hatted swells strutted along Fifth Avenue while immigrants slept in shifts in overcrowded tenements. At night, armies of beggars and streetwalkers accosted anyone and everyone.

But beyond all its commerce and prestige, beyond all its Astor high society and its striving immigrants, it was an open secret that New York City was also the vice capital of the United States. There were 40,000 prostitutes working the streets, charging from 50-

cents to $10 a session. Three vast red-light districts — the Lower East Side, the Washington Square area and the Tenderloin from 23rd to 42nd Street along Broadway — operated discreetly but openly. Peddlers sold pornographic post cards, and dealers trafficked in raunchy Edison wax cylinders of audio smut.

New York City — then composed mainly of Manhattan, with no Brooklyn, Queens or Staten Island — was a pleasure-seekers' paradise: a decadent good-time, hard-drinking city. And all of it was made possible by the corrupt, look-the-other-way connivance of the police force and of corrupt Tammany Hall politicians. Police captains shook down brothel madams for big monthly payoffs; corner cops took bribes from bootblacks wanting choice locations and from fruit vendors who wanted to display wares on the sidewalk. The captains of the New York City Police Department in the era before the Mafia were the ones who "organized" crime in their precincts and settled turf disputes.

New York City was certainly a wicked place, full of temptations. Tourists and out-of-town businessmen flocked there. That is, until Teddy Roosevelt stepped in. When Theodore Roosevelt was commissioner, he tried to enforce all the laws and all police conduct rules, to the absolute shock of most New Yorkers. Roosevelt also wanted officers to be courteous to citizens, a concept almost unthinkable at the time. He tried to shut the saloons on Sunday in strict observance of the Sabbath Excise Law, which got him hated by the vast population of beer-drinking, six-day-a-week workingmen.

He made special efforts to have fair elections; he helped re-introduce the bigger, more fearsome police night stick, and in September 1895, he and the board pioneered a pistol shooting range. Some police historians credit Roosevelt's practice range as leading to the founding of the first police academy. Roosevelt's emphasis on police professionalism and training had its growing pains. Just as Londoners in Peel's time had concerns about a professional police force turning into an army of occupation, Roosevelt's new and improved professionally trained New York City Police Department evoked the same fears. The problem was that militarization and training are synonymous. Effective militaries are always well trained

In the years leading up to, during, and following the United States' 1917 entrance into World War I, the NYPD's transition from the hulking 19th century bruisers of Gangs of New York to modern police officers was cemented by how preparedness and militarization effected the way NYPD officers acted, looked, and understood their jobs. From 1915 through 1917, "preparedness" became a central tenet of Police Commissioner Arthur Woods' department, whether it be for "fire, flood, cyclone, tidal wave, earthquake, or even foreign invasion." Of course, preparing a police force for a foreign invasion also meant remaking it as a military force to be reckoned with.

Many New Yorkers looked on with anxiety as preparedness transformed the NYPD into what resembled a militarized occupation of the city. In one training exercise, police were sent to Staten Island in companies of 350 men, given military rifles and tactics training, and forced to defend a fort during a "sham battle." On October 17, 1916, the NYPD paraded down Fifth Avenue in a fashion they had never done before. Gone were the signature blue uniforms, or the batons hanging from their belt. Now, New Yorkers saw their neighborhood police officers clad in khaki military-style uniforms with rifles on their shoulders and mounted machine guns being pulled on tripods.

As men and as consumers, police were forced to perform preparedness in ways that effected both their wallets and their waistlines. It was during the years leading up to the U.S. entrance into World War I that gymnasiums were built in stationhouses around the city and department administrators obsessively attempted to manage the physique of their officers. Requiring police to cultivate slimmer more disciplined bodies served the dual function of demonstrating a more soldierly appearance while simultaneously promoting food rationing as healthy and eventually, patriotic.

In the first days of January 1917 NYPD designated recruits were made part of the experimental Diet Squad. These husky police officers in training were mandated to live off 25-cents a day. In their daily newspapers, New Yorkers read about the public weigh-ins, meals, and exercise regimens of the men of the Diet Squad. Although the men ultimately gained rather than lost weight, the public attention heaped on the squad's members still succeeded in promoting one message: rationing food doesn't mean starving or even sacrificing.

The first New York City Police Academy opened in 1909 at 240 Centre Street in Manhattan. This location was the new police headquarters and for over sixty-four years, police officers called it the big white castle, the nerve center of the nation's largest and most sophisticated police department. Over the years, the New York City Police Department's Centre Street headquarters would combat mobsters, bootleggers, jewel thieves and serial killers.

Built by the architectural firm: Hoppin, Koen and Huntington for approximately $750,000, Old Police Headquarters, or the Central Office as it was once called, represented one of the most beautiful Beaux-Arts masterpieces Manhattan had to offer. Built between 1905 and 1909 on a wedge-shaped parcel of land bounded by Grand, Centre and Broome Streets where the old Centre Market had stood since 1817, the new headquarters was needed following the consolidation of the five boroughs in 1898, when the police force quadrupled in size.

On midnight November 29, 1909, Police Commissioner William F. Baker inaugurated New York's era of scientific policing when telephone switchboards at the old police headquarters at 300 Mulberry were simultaneously shut down and transferred to the new Central Office. On the first floor of 240 Centre Street, visitors would find an ornate reception room. To the left of reception, guests could find the Chief Inspector's office, the Bureau of Information and the

Boiler Squad, an NYPD unit responsible for testing steam heaters in buildings throughout the city.

Housed on the fourth floor, the City's Police Academy operated at 240 Centre street until it moved to 400 Broome Street in 1928. The facilities included a gym, a drill room, heavy bags and a running track. The cellar boasted a pistol shooting range, the property clerk, and 72 cells for high profile Detective Bureau prisoners. The cellar also contained a deep, dark secret.

According to popular lore, a tunnel was bored to connect Callahan's (now called ONieals) with Police HQ, thereby creating easy passage for the Boys in Blue to enjoy a drink during the trying days of Prohibition. ONieals (the official spelling deprives it of two apostrophes) was established as Callahan's around 1880. The tunnel, while providing undetected access for cop drinking, is now part of the wine cellar. An upstairs brothel held court at one point, and the joint was run as a speakeasy during the dry years. The NYPD headquarters was eventually retired in 1973, leaving the property in vacancy for the next decade.

The tunnel is still visible in ONieals and is used today as the wine cellar. In 1987, the headquarters was sold, turned into luxury residential condos and the tunnel was filled. These luxury condos, commissioned as an NYC landmark, housed some well-known names including Steffi Graf, Winona Ryder and Christi Turlington. The Police Department officially closed 240 Centre Street in 1973, moving headquarters to One Police Plaza. In a testament to the stupidity of the city bureaucracy, rather than relocating the historic records into an archive, the Department unceremoniously dumped a half-century worth of police records into the East River.

During the twentieth century, up until 1964, the New York City Police Academy had several homes including 400 Broome Street, 72 Poplar Street, and 7 Hubert Street. The Broome Street location was located across from Police Headquarters on Centre Street, and it had a particularly interesting history as a police training facility.

For years on St. Patrick's Day, I liked to watch *Three Cheers for the Irish*, a corny 1940 movie about a New York City cop who is forced into retirement to make room for a rookie. The movie indicates that the rookie recently graduated the Police College. For years, I just assumed that New York City Police College was just another example of Hollywood making little attempt to "get it right" regarding the technical aspects of the film. Then, a couple of years ago, I made an amazing discovery (amazing at least for me). There really was a Police College.

In September 1929 the New York City Board of Estimate and Apportionment approved the lease of a building on Broome Street, across from Police Headquarters. The building became known as the Police Headquarters Annex and the Police College occupied the fourth, fifth, and sixth floors.

The Police College was state of the art for the time, with twenty-nine classrooms equipped with portable projectoscopes, stereopticon slides, and motion pictures. There were facilities for Motor Transport School, Horsemanship School, Traffic and Street Safety School, and Detective School, as well as a Recruit Training School. In the New York City Police College annual report of 1930, the police recruit training experience is described as follows:

Getting on the Force of the New York Police Department requires such a high standard of physical and mental ability, that the young officers of the New York Police Department are representative today of the nation's best manhood. The young candidates come from all over the country. A year's residence in New York City is required, then ages must not exceed twenty-nine and weight not less than 140 pounds. The physical examination is very rigid. Not only must the entrant be physically perfect, but he must succeed in a very difficult mental examination. In a word the embryo police officer must possess a well-rounded capacity to cope with all situations developing during his tour of duty.

After passing the required civil service examination, he is turned over to the recruit division of the department, where he is "manufactured" into a policeman by the most scientific methods. He takes a pledge of office, is given a shield and then entered in the Recruits Training School for a ninety-day, intensive course in training.

The course in physical training makes the recruits a good athlete, hardening their muscles, improving their wind, rounding them out as examples of modern police methods of preparing a man for a life job. The mental examination means going to high school all over again. The rookie must study the fundamental purpose of a police department and the part it plays in a town or city where citizens band together in co-operative ways for the advancement of each through the improvement of all. The Rookie must study all penal statutes, the reason for their existence, and the proper way of enforcement. He is also taught the relationship of the police department to all other branches of city service.

As the "Rookie" goes along, dividing his day between calisthenics, wrestling, jiu jitsu exercises and academic instruction in the subjects already mentioned he gets an idea of the wide range of training which is necessary to make a competent police officer. He sees that being a "cop" is more than a job. It is a profession which requires training, physical and mental, that is seldom demanded in any other lines of civilian endeavor. The city takes him over as her ward, looks after his health, helps him to improve his mental status, and gives him an entirely different viewpoint of the policeman in his relationship to citizens and laws. The making of a policeman means the re-making of the man. There is no man who would not be better for taking the rigid police "rookie" course. The handling of himself not only as an individual policeman, but also as a member of a larger group in the handling of meetings, strikes and parades is explained in detail. The student is also taught how to handle himself at fires, to turn in the alarm, to establish fire lines, to clear traffic at fire hydrants, and in general to co-operate most effectively with the fire department.

The average "rookie" has little knowledge of firearms, and great care is exercised to instruct the men in the construction, care and use of the service revolvers. Marksmanship is taught, as well as the method of handling an emergency, and the best way of disarming criminals.

To give a man a police badge, a revolver, and the backing of the entire police department, as well as the city and the courts is a very serious responsibility. The newly approved man goes on the street armed with authority. The moment he separates himself from his squad and starts to patrol his beat he is a complete police department within himself with far-reaching authority. Modern police work requires that the man possess a comprehensive viewpoint of the entire plan of police procedure. He must be able to settle street brawls without the necessity of arrest, to see that the streets he is patrolling are not littered with refuse, to watch the children carefully and to protect them from any harmful street contacts. Not only must he take the brawler and the thug into custody, but he must report to his commanding officer any matters that might require attention from other departments of the city government.

It is necessary that a police officer possess a comprehensive and accurate knowledge of government. He is the representative of organized authority. He is the police representative of every citizen with whom he comes into contact on the street. They have delegated to him the power to enforce law and order as outlined by themselves. While a policeman is trained to be an integral part of a large unit, acting as such while on post he is an individualist of the most pronounced type. He has been taught certain rules and regulations to which he must rigidly conform. Moreover, in a critical situation, his intelligence and his courage often stand between the criminal and the law abiding citizen. "He is faithful unto death." On his ability to use proper judgment rests the honor of the department and the city. The Police College courses of instruction have been planned to make each man more capable as an upstanding, vigorous man and as a representative of modern law and order. He is being taught, not only repressive, but also preventive police work, in order to make him an efficient police officer. His personal efficiency increases respect for law, and in the same ratio decreases the volume of crime. Present and prospective criminals will shun the policeman who is the product of modern training methods. It would be utopian to expect the beginning of a scientific training course in police work to bring about immediate results. Criminals will always be with us. But only through such effective work as the College is doing can we hope to train the men of the department to be better officers and better citizens.

In 1964 the Police Academy moved to 235 East 20th Street in the Grammercy Park section of Manhattan. This is the facility I came to know as the Academy, or as the staff called it – Club 235.

In another example of New York City bureaucracy at its best, New York City Mayor Ed Koch declared the 20th Street Academy outdated and obsolete in 1989. It wasn't until almost two decades later that a new Police Academy complex opened in College Point, Queens.

Wait a minute! I was a member of the New York City Transit Police Department, right? So, what did my experience have to do with the New York City Police Academy? To understand that phenomenon, you have to understand some of the history of policing in New York City.

For the better part of the twentieth century the City of New York had been policed by three separate and distinct police departments – the New York City Police Department, the New York City Transit Police Department, and the New York City Housing Police Department. Since 1964 the three departments had the same rank structure and the pay and benefits were almost identical. Police officers in all the departments wore identical uniforms, with the exception of the department shoulder patch. While the NYPD policed the streets of the city, the Transit Police was responsible for policing the subway system, and the Housing Police handled the City's public housing projects. I had been appointed to the Transit Police Department in 1981 and almost every subsequent year there had been talk of a police merger in the city, but the talk always seemed to just fade away. In 1994, however, merging the Transit and Housing departments into the NYPD became a pet project of

Mayor Rudolph Giuliani. The merger talks dragged on for about a year until the mayor played a trump card that had never been used in years past. The Metropolitan Transportation Authority was the New York State public authority that controlled and financed the Transit Police Department, and the MTA had no intention of ending its control of the department. The City of New York, however, contributed approximately $50 million each year for the operation of the Transit Police. The mayor simply put forth a very basic proposal. The MTA could keep the Transit Police Department, but they would have to do it without the City's $50-million annual contribution. Faced with this new economic reality the MTA was not so eager to have its own police department, and the MTA Board quickly voted to approve the police merger. On April 2, 1995 the Transit Police Department ceased to exist followed shortly thereafter by the dissolution of the Housing Police Department. But what about all those years when three distinct departments existed. Where were the police academies for the Transit and Housing Departments? While there were separate training academies in operation at times, the New York City Police Academy was something of a "Mother Ship" for training in all three departments. Since I was originally a transit cop, I would be remiss if I did not make mention of the Transit Police Department and the Transit Police Academies that operated throughout the life of the agency.

    Rapid transit has played an integral part in the lives of New Yorkers for well over 100 years. The first trains ran at grade level and on elevated structures. Underground trains were added on

October 27, 1904 when, after taking four and a half years to build, the Interborough Rapid Transit (IRT) opened to the public. Since both the IRT and the competing BMT (Brooklyn-Manhattan Transit) lines were privately financed and built, they had no police, in lieu of their own private security personnel. The new IND (Independent) lines, however, which began operating in 1932, were owned by New York City and run by the Board of Transportation. These lines originally had "station supervisors" employed to police them, their names having been taken from the NYC Police Department's hiring list.

On November 17, 1933, six men were sworn in as New York State Railway Police. They were unarmed but were still responsible for the safety of the passengers on the IND line as well as guarding the system's property. Two years later, twenty "station supervisors, class B" were added for police duty. Responsible for assisting in the opening and closing of doors and announcing destinations, these twenty-six "specials" were soon given powers of arrest.

Beginning in 1949, the question as to who should supervise the Transit Police Department was one which was carefully scrutinized over the next five years by various city officials. The issue being considered was, "Should Transit be taken over by the NYPD?" In 1955, the decision was made that the Transit Police Department would become a separate and distinctly different Department, ending almost two decades of rule by the NYPD. The Civil Service Commission established a new test for transit recruits, and on April 4, the first appointments from the list were made. An NYPD lieutenant, Thomas O'Rourke, was also designated the first commanding officer of the Transit Police Department. Soon after, Lieutenant O'Rourke along with nine others, passed the captain's exam. Captain O'Rourke was then appointed as the first Chief of the new department.

With crime on the rise, the number of transit officers increased so that by 1966, the Department had grown to 2,272 officers. That year, Robert H. Rapp was appointed Chief by the NYC Transit Authority. Under Chief Rapp, and at the direction of the Mayor, an ambitious new anti-crime program got underway. The program had a goal of assigning an officer to each of New York City's subway trains between the hours of 8:00 PM and 4:00 AM. And the Transit Police Department continued to grow. By early 1975, the department comprised nearly 3,600 members.

In 1975, a former NYPD chief inspector and sometime City Council president, Sanford D. Garelik, was appointed Chief of the Transit Police Department. Determined to reorganize the Transit Police Department, Chief Garelik was also successful in instilling a new sense of pride and professionalism among the ranks. However, the fiscal crisis that began that year was an unexpected blow - especially to transit cops. Over the next five years, layoffs and attrition would reduce their numbers to fewer than 2,800. New officers would not be hired until 1980. By the early 1990's however, the Transit Police Department had regained all of its former strength and had increased even further.

In 1991 the Transit Police gained national accreditation under Chief William Bratton. The Department became one of only 175 law enforcement agencies in the country and only the second in the New York State to achieve that distinction. The following year it was also accredited by the State of New York, and by 1994, there were almost 4,500 uniformed and civilian members of the Department, making it the sixth largest police force in the United States.

Over time, however, the separation between the NYPD and the NYC Transit Police Department created more and more problems. Redundancy of units, difficulty in communications and differences in procedures all created frustration and inefficiency. As part of his mayoral campaign, candidate Rudolph Giuliani pledged to end the long unresolved discussion and merge all three of New York City's police departments into a single, coordinated force. Mayor Giuliani took office on January 1, 1994, and immediately undertook to fulfill his promise and end a problem that had defied final solution for almost half a century. Discussions between the City and the New York City Transit Authority produced a memorandum of understanding, and on April 2, 1995, the NYC Transit Police was consolidated with the New York City Police Department to become a new Bureau within the NYPD. After a reorganization of the Department in February of 1997, the Transit Bureau became the

Transit Division within the newly formed Transportation Bureau. The Transportation Bureau dissolved in the Spring of 1998 and in July of 1999, the Transit Division once again became the Transit Bureau.

From the 50s to the 70's the Transit Police Academy operated in Queens, first out of the Jamaica Armory and then the Flushing Armory. The academy then relocated to 300 Gold Street in Brooklyn. The 1974 class at the Gold Street academy had the distinction of being the last class to be hired with the title of Patrolman rather than Police Officer.

The 1974 class was the last year recruits received their firearms at the beginning of training as opposed to just before graduation. Prior to 1974, recruits of all three police departments were issued their guns and shields a few days into academy training. Background investigations were not extensive then, and I have spoken to some real old timers who recall some pretty wild academy episodes during that era. There were stories of recruits frisking one another in academy hallways with their revolvers drawn and cocked. There was even an incident where a couple of recruits held up a bank. As a police academy instructor from the era eloquently stated, "You had a better chance of getting killed in the academy than you did in the street." Even when firearms stopped being issued at the beginning of training, there was still a period of time when recruits received their shields right after being hired. It took a tragic mishap to put the finishing touches on the tradition of gun & shield day, where both are issued just before graduation.

A few nights after orientation, a student officer in possession of his newly issued police shield was in a bar in Bay Ridge, Brooklyn, when a melee erupted outside. The recruit ran outside to break up the fight with his shield in his outstretched hand, shouting: "Police!" He was grabbed and beaten by a small mob. As he lay on the ground gasping and begging for mercy, the mob stomped on him. Injuring him fatally.

When hiring began again after the fiscal crisis, the Transit Police recruits trained at the NYPD Police Academy, but they were not mixed with NYPD recruits. The Transit Police Academy ran its own operation. When I was hired by the Transit Police Department in 1981 the Transit Police Academy moved to 155th Street and 8th Avenue in Manhattan. This location had been a public grammar school and was another temporary location used during 1981 and 1982. In 1983 training for the NYPD, Transit and Housing Departments was conducted together at the NYPD Academy. The tri-agency training continued until 1993 when the Transit Police opened their own Academy back at 300 Gold Street. The separate Transit Police Academy lasted for only two years. The police merger in 1995 eliminated the Transit and Housing departments, with all police recruits being trained back at the New York City Police Academy. As far as the Housing Police Department went, my research found very little in the way of a specific Housing Police

Academy. This is in no way meant to be a slight to my Hosing Police brethren, but the only reference I could find was the mention of a Housing Police Academy on Water Street after the department was established in 1952.

The academy experiences in this book occurred during the 1980s and 90s. It should be noted that NYPD training has changed substantially over the years. The NYPD Police Academy trains approximately 4,000 recruits each year in two classes of about 2,000 recruits each. The academy has five sections that conduct different aspects of training: Recruit Training, Firearms and Tactics, Specialized Training, Leadership Development, and Executive Development. Recruit training is divided into two terms that together encompass 23 weeks: Knowledge and Fitness and Skills and Abilities. The Patrol Services, Housing, and Transit Bureaus are responsible for in-service training, including the Field Training Program for new probationary police officers after they graduate from the Police Academy. In-service training occurs through a number of different vehicles. The most structured forms of regular in-service training are borough-based (or "IN-TAC") training, precinct-level training, and semiannual firearm-requalification training.

The new, integrated recruit curriculum takes a holistic approach to police training. Police Academy instructors are generalists, able to impart to the new recruits the knowledge and skills needed to be an effective police officer. The unified curriculum draws on three main traditional areas of police training: Law, Police Science and Behavioral Science. Unlike the past, when each discipline was taught independently, the new curriculum has been updated to reflect the changing role of police officers in today's society. Police officers are expected to play the role of social worker, crime fighter, mediator, first responder, teacher and role model to name a few. As such, police officers are required to learn and be able to apply the law and patrol guide procedures as well as have the emotional competence to carry out their role effectively. While in the academy, recruit officers are expected to acquire a working knowledge of the law and its various components, such as: search and seizure, rights of people taken into custody, laws of arrest, criminal procedure law and the guidelines on the use of deadly physical force. In addition, they are instructed on Police Department policies, procedures, regulations and tactics; these include: and introduction to law enforcement, the Police Department's mission and rank structure, report writing, emergencies and unusual disorders, arrest procedures and many more. These technical skills, coupled with further instruction on effective communication, ethics, crisis intervention and the ability to appreciate other cultures form the basis of the new, unified curriculum. A variety of approaches are used to teach the recruit officers. Aside from the traditional classroom format, instructors employ role-plays and socio-dramas, simulations and assessment exercises, team teaching, tutoring and other student centered methodologies. This helps bridge the gap between theory and practice and affords the recruit officers the opportunity to practice their newly acquired knowledge and skills. Instructors have supervisory roles and responsibilities relative to their recruit officers. The discretion and latitude enjoyed by an instructor is an awesome responsibility and is viewed as an opportunity to expand skills while shaping the future of the Department.

CHAPTER 3: GRABBING MY RUBBER BAND

During the mid-1970's New York City experienced a devastating financial crisis in which the city nearly went bankrupt. Thousands of city workers, including police officers from all three departments were laid off. Slowly, financial conditions improved and the laid off workers were brought back. In 1979, the Police Academy went back into the business of training new recruits. During 1979 and 1980, Transit Police recruits were also trained at the New York City Police Academy, but the operations of NYPD and TPD were separate. NYPD recruits and instructors worked during the day tour while Transit staff and recruits worked 4PM x 12AM.

It was during 1980 that I took the civil service exam for Transit Police Officer. I scored 98% on the exam, and all my subsequent processing involved the NYPD and the New York City Police Academy. My physical agility test was at the Police Academy, as was my medical exam. When I finally was notified that I was being hired, my swearing in ceremony was at NYPD Headquarters. I just assumed that my Police Academy experience would be at "The" Police Academy on 20th Street. What I was woefully unaware of, however, was all the politics playing out behind the scenes.

As the financial situation in the city became better, all the departments began cranking up their hiring and training of police officers. Traditionally, the NYPD ran two, six-month training sessions for recruits – a class in January and a class in July. There was a magic number designated for a recruit class. Once the magic number was passed, the academy had to work in two squads with training taking place during days and evenings. Police hirings became so extensive during the late 80s and early 90s that there were times the academy went to three squads, with training taking place 24/7.

During the time I was getting ready to be hired by the Transit Police, the NYPD was using their academy on the 4PM x 12AM shift, so there was no room to place a transit class of recruits. The lack of facilities appeared to be a moot point. There had been a lawsuit filed claiming that the Transit Police Officer civil service exam I had taken was discriminatory to minorities, and a judge had granted an injunction. That was just great! I scored 98% on the test, completed all the other required testing and background checks, and now the list was apparently dead. But then in October of 1981 a judge unexpectedly lifted the injunction. The Transit Police Department had to act fast before another injunction could be put in place. 420 Transit Police Officers were hired – a huge class by Transit Police standards. There was just one problem now. Where was the police academy going to be?

After the swearing in ceremony, my class was directed to report the following day to a Transit Police facility at 300 Gold Street in downtown Brooklyn. The four days at Gold Street was mostly "hurry up and wait". We were spread out throughout the building in every office and room where a chair could be found. Once in a while a uniformed police officer or sergeant would come in and speak about the academy curriculum, and at other times we would walk a few blocks in small groups to the Transit Authority headquarters on Jay Street to fill out numerous forms and to have ID photos taken. Mostly, however, we just sat in our assigned rooms. On Friday afternoon, just before dismissal for the weekend, a sergeant entered my room, and directed us to report to a New York City public high school on Adelphi Street in Brooklyn at 4PM on Monday. No other information was offered. We all went home for the weekend wondering if the school on Adelphi Street was our police academy.

We were required to work 4:00 PM x 12:00 AM at the school on Adelphi Street for a good reason. The building was an active high school and high school classes with a full student body were taking place during the day. During the week at the high school we were finally able to begin the police academy curriculum, which included training in police science, social science, law, physical training and defensive tactics. By Friday night we were settling into the routine when the entire class was summoned into the school auditorium just before our midnight off duty time. A sergeant made the announcement. It was time for our nomadic tribe to fold up our tents and move on. This time, we were directed to report on Monday morning at 7:00 AM to 155th Street and 8th Ave in Manhattan to our latest police academy.

The weekend found me struggling to contain my excitement. Perhaps the confusion of the first two weeks had been necessary to put the finishing touches on a brand new, modern police training facility. And I knew all about a state-of-the-art law enforcement training academy. Approximately three years earlier I had been hired as a Border Patrol Agent and spent 16-weeks training at the Border Patrol Academy at the Federal Law Enforcement Training Center in Georgia.

The Federal Law Enforcement Training Center (FLETC) serves as an interagency law enforcement training body for 91 federal law enforcement agencies. It also provides training to state, local, campus, tribal, and international law enforcement agencies.

The FLETC headquarters are at the former Naval Air Station in the Glynco area of unincorporated Glynn County, Georgia, near the port city of Brunswick, Georgia, and about halfway between Savannah, Georgia and Jacksonville, Florida. Studies conducted in the late 1960s revealed an urgent need for training by professional instructors using modern training facilities and standardized course content. The permanent location of the center was originally planned for the Washington, D.C. area. However, a three-year construction delay resulted in Congress requesting that surplus federal installations be surveyed to determine if one could serve as the permanent site. In May 1975, after a review of existing facilities, the Glynco site was selected. In the summer of 1975, the new Federal Law Enforcement Training Center relocated from Washington, D.C., and began training in September of that year at Glynco. The facility was just over three years old when twenty Border Patrol trainees arrived from Chula Vista and were joined by twelve trainees from El Paso to form the 128th session of the United States Border Patrol Academy.

To a kid from New York City, the center appeared to be mostly a heavily wooded forest. Spread out among the 1,600 acres were the facilities, including buildings for administration, classrooms and training, dining, dormitories, instructor offices, gymnasium, student center, convenience store, auditorium, outdoor firing range, driver training range, swimming pool and athletic field. Despite the rural setting, the training facilities were state of the art for the time. This modern training environment contributed greatly to my culture shock when I began training at my first police academy in New York City.

I was still very excited early Monday morning as I rode the D train uptown to 155th Street. I was not at all familiar with the area, but I had read that the location was known as Coogan's Bluff, and for 83-years it had been the site of the Polo Grounds, the home of the old New York Giants baseball team. The Mets played at the Polo

Grounds during their first two seasons, and I still had a very vague memory of attending a game there with my father and grandfather during 1963, its last year of use.

As I ascended the subway steps, I thought of the many thousands of baseball fans who climbed these same steps on their way to a ball game. There was no baseball at Coogan's Bluff, however. For many years the landscape had been dominated by the hi-rise buildings of a New York City public housing project.

I looked across 8th Avenue and was immediately disappointed. I saw nothing resembling a modern, contemporary, state-of-the-art police training facility. Facing me was an old, antiquated, New York City public school. Further investigation revealed the two-story brick building had been a public grammar school several years earlier, so it was no surprise that the classrooms were filled with desks appropriate for the size of the average grade school student.

The chipped paint, filthy windows, and patches of graffiti spread liberally throughout the halls painted an obvious picture that this school had been closed for several years. The gym was so small that it was impossible to run in company formation during physical training. For this activity we were mustered outside to a concrete playground/athletic field typically found attached to NYC public schools.

The high portion of 155th Street started on the West Side at Riverside Drive, crossing Broadway, Amsterdam Avenue, and Saint Nicholas Avenue. At Saint Nicholas Place, the terrain dropped off steeply, forming Coogan's Bluff. 155th Street was carried on a 1,600-foot long viaduct, a City Landmark constructed in 1893, that sloped down towards the Harlem River, continuing onto the Macombs Dam Bridge, crossing over the Harlem River Drive. By standing on this elevated viaduct, a person could look directly down onto our concrete field. Word of our arrival must have spread pretty quickly, because by the third day of academy classes, companies running in formation in the concrete field were being pelted by bricks and bottles from the elevated roadway. For the duration of the academy class a uniformed police officer had to be posted on the viaduct during academy class hours.

This truly was an awful facility, but as training got underway, the Transit Police Department actually found ways to make conditions worse. My class of 420 recruits filled the building, but conditions were not overly crowded. I guess the Department felt we had it too easy so two months after my class was hired approximately two hundred additional recruits were hired and jammed into our academy building. Now, conditions were overcrowded. As a matter of fact, the building was bursting at the seams with police recruits. For the first two months of training recruits were able to go into a locker room to change in and out of physical training uniforms, and there was access to showers. Those locker rooms had now been transitioned into classrooms, so while the female recruits changed in the ladies rooms, the males changed at their desks in their classrooms. With no showers, as the weeks progressed those classrooms became pretty ripe after gym class. Whenever I would change back into recruit uniform and sit in my own sweat I would shake my head and think back a couple of years to physical training at FLETC. Each day my Border Patrol recruit class would march to the free-standing state-of the-art gymnasium. On the way to the locker room we would pass a counter where a worker would hand out gym uniforms for the day. That's right – every day we were issued a fresh gym uniform. After showering and dressing we would throw our soiled gym gear in a laundry bag as we exited the building.

Do you think having bricks and bottles thrown at you and having to wallow in your own sweat all day is enough? Hold on! Believe it or not, conditions got worse. The boiler in the building didn't work. My class was hired in October, so the lack of heat wasn't apparent for the first two months. As the New York City winter began to move in during December, the lack of heat became painfully obvious. It took threats from the Patrolman's Benevolent Association to go to court to have the site condemned before the Department finally had the boiler repaired.

As a fitting postscript for this atrocious facility, once the recruits hired two months after my class had graduated, the building was turned over to the New York City Department of Homeless Services. Nevertheless, Harlem High or University, as it was affectionately known by the two classes that passed through its doors, was our police academy, and will forever occupy a special place in my heart.

I have to admit that as a freshly graduated police officer, I was not enamored with life in the Transit Police Department. I knew that being a police officer would involve working hours around the clock, but when my class graduated, we were all assigned to the newly created Tactical Patrol Force. The name of the unit sounded impressive, but all it consisted of was train patrol from 8PM to 4AM. To make matters worse, we were forced to work our first regular day off, so instead of four days on two days off, the duty chart became five days on one day off. If this happened to me ten years later, I probably would have had a completely different perspective. If I was married with kids and a mortgage, I would have drooled at the idea of overtime pay every week, but when I was assigned to TPF I was single and living at home. The schedule threw my entire life upside down.

Thankfully, I was only on TPF for six months. Being totally honest, if I had to remain on TPF for a longer period of time, I'm pretty sure my career would have worked out much differently. I was never going to quit, but I definitely would have looked for another law enforcement job. As it was, I was called for a job as a New York State Court Officer, and as tempting as it was to get off TPF, the Court Officer exam had been tied up in litigation, so I was being offered a provisional appointment. If it was decided that the exam had been discriminatory and had to be given over again, I would have to take the test like everyone else and score high enough to get hired. I did not hate TPF that much to take such a risk.

I was finally able to transfer to District 4 in Union Square, Manhattan. I was assigned to a rotating squad and changed shifts every week. This might not seem desirous, but after six months of steady 8PM x 4AM I considered rotating to be heaven.

I settled into life in the district, and I enjoyed the work and the camaraderie. The first chance I had to become cynical occurred when I had about four years on the job. Transit policing was almost exclusively foot patrol, and I had bought into management's mantra that the most important factor for a good patrol cop was to be visible – to be out there where the public could see you. That's exactly what I did – I was out there. I wasn't hiding or sleeping in rooms. I wrote my summonses and made arrests when something happened in front of me, but I was far from what would be considered a heavy collar man. In other words, I didn't make a lot of arrests. So, after four years of doing the job I was looking for something new to advance my career. I applied for the plainclothes task force, which in the Transit Police was the path to a detective's gold shield. It still stings when I think about the three-person interview panel of task force superior officers. They basically told me that I had some nerve to waste their time, forcing them to interview someone who didn't have impressive arrest numbers. I only made the situation worse when I expressed my opinion that the effectiveness of uniformed patrol cannot be judged on arrest numbers. Needless to say, I left that interview completely deflated. As weeks passed, my moribund mood worsened with some of the accomplishments college friends were making. One had graduated law school, and another just passed his CPA exam. At the time, the only education requirement necessary to become a police officer was a high school diploma. Some of my college friends would rib me about wasting my time, money, and effort to obtain a four-year college degree only to become a cop. I was beginning to think they might be right.

One summer night I entered the district early before a midnight shift. After I changed into uniform, I sat in the muster room and flipped through the pages of the clipboard containing department bulletins. One bulletin in particular caught my eye. It was a position vacancy announcement for police academy instructors. The thought of being an instructor had never entered my mind, but as I read the bulletin, I noticed that the only formal requirement for the position was a four-year college degree. Just on general principle I had to apply. Finally, my degree qualified me for something on this job. I filled out the application and went back to rotating life in District 4. Several weeks later I was notified to report to the Transit Police facility at Gold Street in Brooklyn for the interview for the instructor position. It wasn't so much an interview as it was a test.

I was taken to a classroom where the only other occupant was a police officer standing behind a video camera on a tripod. The camera operator motioned for me to select one of the ten blank index cards that were laid out on the desk in the front of the room. I picked up a card and turned it over, revealing the word "Sock". The cameraman stated, "Collect your thoughts and in 30-seconds I will turn on the camera. You have to talk for five minutes on your selected word."

With the enthusiasm of a Hollywood director, the cop pointed towards me. "Action!"

After a slight hesitation, I was off and running. I talked about different types of socks, the reasons to wear socks, and I even drew and labeled a diagram of a sock on the blackboard. I realized that I still had at least two minutes remaining, so I switched context. I talked about how sock was also analogous to striking someone. For my grand finale, I pointed out how "sock" was one of the standard words that appeared on the screen during a fight scene on the Batman TV show to indicate that Batman had just punched one of the villains. The cameraman shouted, "Cut!" just as I finished my Batman speech. I had nailed the timing perfectly. I may not have made many arrests, but I could sure talk about socks. The cameraman cop escorted me to another office where I was interviewed by a lieutenant. Interview was actually much too strong a word. The lieutenant looked over my application to ensure that he could read my handwriting before sending me on my way back to District 4. I didn't know what to think, but I felt a degree of satisfaction on the train ride back to Manhattan. At least my college degree had qualified me for consideration for the position.

Several months passed and I just assumed police academy instructor would not be in the cards for me. One day in mid-December, I entered the district at the end of a day tour and walked past the roll call area on the way to the locker room. Mickey, a veteran cop assigned to roll call yelled out, "Hey professor!"

I kept walking toward the locker room until a cop passing me in the other direction pointed to Mickey and said, "I think he's talking to you."

I wheeled around and observed Mickey beckoning me toward his desk. "Hey professor," he said. "You've been transferred to the Police Academy. Report tomorrow morning at 0700 to the NYPD Police Academy."

I shrugged. "OK," I said while continuing toward the locker room. Reality didn't set in until the administrative sergeant approached my locker and told me to make sure my locker was cleaned out within a week, because they needed the lockers for incoming personnel. I packed up most of my uniforms and equipment and put them in the trunk of my car. When I settled into the driver's seat, I took a deep breath. Oh my God! I was going to be a police academy instructor.

At 6:30 AM the next morning I turned off the sidewalk on East 20th Street, walked across the campus deck and entered through the revolving doors. The Police Academy was an eight-story granite building with a gym annexed to its west border, a building whose classrooms, laboratories, offices, and facilities I would come to know intimately. The academy had a pool, a gym, a cafeteria, and even a museum of the New York City Police Department.

At 7:00 AM I was seated in a classroom with twenty-five other new instructors, eager to begin our missions as police trainers. The first order of business was to complete the two-week Methods of Instruction course so we could at least be marginally functional in a classroom setting. I have to admit I felt a little less special when the sergeant from the Instructor Development Unit explained why we were all assigned to the academy. A very large recruit class would begin in a few weeks requiring significant additions to the instructional staff.

A few years earlier, the era of tri-agency hiring had begun. The Transit and Housing Police Departments no longer administered their own police officer civil service exams, but instead hired from the NYPD exam and list. A simple formula was used for hiring. For every ten police officers hired, seven went to NYPD, two to Transit and one to Housing. This system of hiring led to some very anxious moments for new recruits reporting to be sworn in, as they were not told right up until the time of the swearing in which department they were being hired for. The same system was used for Police Academy instructional staff. To supplement the NYPD personnel, there had to be a certain amount of Transit and Housing instructors detailed to the NYPD academy. So, as I sat in MOI on that first morning among seven other Transit Police new instructors, I understood the reality of my selection. It wasn't because of the magnificent manner in which I presented "Sock." It was because I had the prerequisite college degree and they needed the body to fulfill their quota of instructors to the NYPD.

Regardless of the fact that I was chosen simply as a warm body to fill a vacancy, I was an instructor at the New York City Police Academy, and I was determined to make the most of this opportunity. The sergeant from the Instructor Development Unit who gave the opening address to the class provided an instant stroke to my ego. Salesmen love me because I've always been susceptible to a good line of shit, and this guy was stellar. His speech went something like this:

Throughout our lives, from our parents to our teachers, role models and mentors help us pick the right paths and make the right choices. The same is true in the NYPD. From the first day these recruits enter the Police Academy, their mentors are the instructors whose job it is to transform them from raw recruits to qualified police officers. The formal aspect of the academy training process requires rookies to take and pass a specified number of tests, including academic, laws, fitness, and firearms. There is also another, often overlooked, side to the recruit training equation — the informal training from role models and mentors like you. At many points during their careers, these recruits will face ethical dilemmas, and they will think back to the moral and ethical foundation you provided for them.

The instructor also walked around the room and gave each new instructor a rubber band. He said that police training is something that gets in an instructor's blood, and that regardless of our promotions and assignments, at some point our rubber bands would ultimately pull us back to the Police Academy. I didn't fully grasp the rubber band concept at that time, but the motivational speech had worked on me. Wow – maybe I wasn't just a warm body with a college degree needed to fill a vacancy no one else applied for. Maybe I would be an instrumental force in shaping the careers of new police officers. We'll revisit this premise shortly, but for now, I was off and running with the two weeks designed to make me functional as an instructor.

The MOI class and its instructors were excellent. The program was organized to culminate in the presentation of a 50-minute lesson of instruction, simulating an actual recruit class. During the two weeks we learned about ethical issues in law enforcement training, the principles of adult learning, presentation skills, lesson plan and performance objective development, instructional methodologies, and classroom management. At the end of the two weeks I received a passing grade on my presentation. I was exuberant and all set to get into a classroom with real recruits. The only problem was – what would I be teaching?

The Recruit School of the New York City Police Academy was divided into several disciplines. There were some training disciplines, such as firearms training and driver training, where the recruits traveled off-site for the training. There were four disciplines the recruits received training in daily at the academy for the entire six months – police science, law, social science, and physical training.

During the MOI course, no one ever queried the class as to their preference of assignment. On the last day of the class, the motivational sergeant entered the room - calmly read out the assignments – said good luck and departed. The assignments didn't cause much controversy, but there was some trepidation, including on my part. I had been assigned to the police science department. If I had been given a choice, police science would have been my last selection. The law is the law and dealing with people in a professional manner is universal. There were, however, significant differences in the procedures of the New York City Police Department and the New York City Transit Police Department, and a large portion of the police science curriculum involved procedures. How was I going to teach procedures I had never performed, and in some instances, didn't even know existed? My dilemma, however, was paltry compared to the predicament faced by another new instructor.

The first aspect of being an NYPD Police Academy instructor that shocked me was the experience of the average instructor. The main reason I had considered my acceptance to the academy as being a long shot was my five years on the job. I assumed that instructor roles were generally reserved for salty veterans with far more experience than I possessed. What a surprise to find that I was one of the more senior cops in the MOI class. If my memory is correct, there was a transit cop with fifteen years and an NYPD cop with twelve. The remainder of the class averaged between three and four years of service. Joe was one of the NYPD officers with three years on the job. At the completion of the MOI, Joe was assigned to the physical training department. These instructors taught various physical tactics, such as handcuffing and use of the baton. They also put the recruits through a regimen of calisthenics and running every class. This required the instructor to run and perform the exercises along with the recruits. This was a choice assignment for someone who worked out and ran. Think about it – your primary role at your job is working out. You would never have to work out on your own time. The problem for Joe, however, was that he didn't work out. In fact, he was substantially overweight and feared he would not be able to perform the exercises and running distances the recruits would be required to do.

    Pete, one of the other NYPD cops who had been assigned to the physical training department, and who was in fantastic physical condition, told Joe his condition was not a big deal. Pete said that he knew how the gym classes operated, and that it was only the instructor assigned as the lead instructor for a class who had to perform along with the recruits. He explained that with the recruit class spread out on the gym floor, the lead instructor mounted a large platform and led them in the calisthenics. Pete recommended that whenever Joe was on the platform, he order the recruits to "about face." Then, Joe could stop his personal exercising anytime he fatigued. That seemed too simple, but even if it worked, Joe had another problem. The lead instructor ran at the front of the recruit formation as they circled the outside perimeter of the gym for up to two miles. Joe was pretty sure he couldn't make it two miles and he couldn't order the recruits to run backwards. Pete wasn't fazed by the problem. He told Joe all he had to do was work out some signal with another instructor. After a few laps around the gym, once Joe felt he was fading fast he would give the signal to the instructor who would call out to Joe that there was an important phone call for him in the gym office. I don't know if Joe ever had to use those tricks. The physical training instructors were in their own world and didn't interact daily with the academic instructors. I did notice over the next several months that Joe did drop a significant amount of weight, so in retrospect, Joe's assignment was the best thing for him. As for me, I was faced with the proposition of entering the classroom wearing my Transit Police patch, and instructing the recruits in subjects like the rotation tow program, removal of vehicles from parkways, highways, and expressways, NYPD disciplinary policies, and evictions, repossessions and other civil process – procedures that were not within the scope of the Transit Police Department. Even the topics common to all departments like arrests, discipline, property, summonses, and personnel matters had policies and procedures unique to each department. This was certainly going to be interesting.

Police Academy instructors were usually assigned two companies to teach and were designated as the Official Company Instructor (OCI) for one of the companies. The OCI was responsible for all the administrative details regarding the company. New instructors going through the recruit program for the first time were assigned one company and were not designated as an OCI. My first tour at the NYPD Police Academy was two years and included four academy classes. I was an OCI with two assigned companies for the last three sessions, but by far, my first class, with one company and no OCI duties was the most taxing. The entire six-month class was a race to stay just ahead of my company. Sometimes, I would complete a lesson plan fifteen minutes before I entered the classroom to present the lesson.

On the first day of classes, all the instructors started with the same lesson. In theory, everyone should always have been presenting the same lessons on the same days. In reality, after the first few weeks, companies began to deviate from the academic schedule by design. For example, the first time a company went for a week to the firearms range in Rodman's Neck, it dropped them off the academic pace. My point is that it did not take very long to have companies on different academic schedules. On a particular day one company might be on academic day 32, while the company in the adjacent room is on day 31, and still another company was completing day 34.

It was fairly common during my first recruit class to be assigned to substitute for an instructor of another company. Situations would arise where an instructor would need to take the day off, and the new instructors with one company assigned were the logical choices to cover as opposed to giving a third class to instructors already carrying two daily classes. Subbing was not a big deal. The instructor of the company being covered would leave a note confirming what lesson his/her company was up to. It was always a bonus for me if the company I was covering was behind my company or on the same pace because that meant I already had the necessary lesson plan prepared. If the company was ahead of my class schedule, it meant I had to prepare the lesson plan. Not a big deal because I was going to have to prepare the same lesson plan for my company eventually.

About three weeks into my first class, one of the squad sergeants in the police science department told me I would have to cover a class for the instructor of Company 3 who had to take an emergency excusal. The sergeant told me he had just talked to the instructor and he told me what lesson Company 3 was up to. No big deal. It was the same lesson I was going to present to my Company 7. Instead of going through the material once, I would be presenting it in back to back sessions. When I finished the class with Company 7 I walked down the hall prepared to give an encore performance to

Company 3. I was about a minute into my repeat performance when I noticed the extended hand of the company sergeant. "Sir, we covered this lesson yesterday."

Uh oh! I had not prepared the next lesson yet. As a matter of fact, I didn't even know the subject of the next lesson. I intended to prepare that lesson at my desk when I finished this class. What was I going to do now? Maybe I could use a kindergarten technique and tell the class to put their heads down on the desk and take a nap. No, that solution would likely land me back patrolling a subway platform by the next morning. Maybe I was overblowing the seriousness of my situation. Maybe the next lesson was one of the easy ones that I was already familiar with.

I directed the company sergeant to bring his class schedule to me. I scanned the police science schedule, and to my horror, the lesson scheduled for this class was the rotation tow program, one of those NYPD specific topics a transit cop knew nothing about. I meekly thanked the company sergeant and then opened my patrol guide to the rotation tow section. I took a long look at the recruits assembled before me and took a deep breath. I had to say something. Silently staring at them for the next hour would likely be worse that the nap idea. I opened my mouth hoping something reasonably intelligent would emerge.

"Ingersoll Towing."

There was a pregnant pause while the room of confused faces digested my wisdom. I cleared my throat and hoped I would make some sense. "Ingersoll Towing was a tow company in Southern California. Before I came on this job, I spent two years as a Border Patrol Agent. I was assigned to the San Clemente highway checkpoint station approximately 70-miles north of the Mexican Border. We seized numerous vehicles transporting illegal aliens, and these vehicles eventually had to be towed from our station to several locations based upon whether they were being forfeited, stored as evidence, or eligible for return to owner. We had a list at the station of six authorized tow companies we could call for service, but there was no particular order or rotation mandating when a particular company could be called. All the tow companies were efficient, but whenever Ingersoll Tow was called, the driver would always arrive with a big box of fried chicken for the agents at the station. Who do you think received almost every call for towing service at the San Clemente station?"

There were low chuckles from the class, indicating my point had been made. Now I just had to bring the point home to the current lesson. I pointed to the Transit Police patch on my left sleeve and asked a rhetorical question. "Do you know what this patch is?" I went right on to my next overhead question. "Do you know how many vehicles I've Ro-Towed?" I approached a tall, thin recruit sitting in the front of the second row. "How many do you think I've Ro-Towed?" The recruit fidgeted uncomfortably in his seat and shrugged. I switched back to addressing the entire class. "Let me help you. The answer is none – zero. Transit Police Officers do not get involved with the rotation tow program. Why does the program exist? Because I'm sure the Ingersoll Tow companies of the world are not limited to Southern California." Again, there were muffled snickers from the class. "So, let's go through the procedure together. If I can understand it, so can you."

I was sweating profusely when I left that classroom, but I had pulled it off. I had discovered a very effective and unique instructional tool – honesty. If I tried to go into these classes and convince these recruits that a transit cop was well versed and experienced in these NYPD specific procedures – they would see right through me, and I would be exposed as a phony. To the contrary, honesty really did turn out to be the best policy. For the remainder of my time teaching police science, whenever I came to one of those NYPD specific topics, I had a simple, yet effective mantra. I would explain to the class that obviously, a transit cop would have no experience in the particular subject, but if I could learn the subject to present in class, then they could learn it to do well on a test.

CHAPTER FOUR: THE RISK TAKERS

There is a degree of risk that runs throughout life, and to some degree, we all take risks at one time or another. Some jobs are riskier than others and some people are comfortable being risk-takers. While caution and common sense are paramount concerns in every walk of life, a degree of risk taking is necessary in the police profession. Lives were saved and heroes born from cops taking risks.

Unfortunately, the propensity to take risks was not always positive in nature. Sometimes, cops would risk everything for something completely illogical, yet alluring. One such attraction was as old as time itself. History is replete with men who have taken innumerable risks for women, some to the extent of losing their lives. Romeo, Adam, Sampson, Solomon, and King Edward VIII of England are among those who demonstrated that though powerful in their own rights, the loving attention from the right woman was sufficient to easily bring them to their knees, and in some cases, to their graves.

In more recent times, an admitted affair crumbled the career of CIA Director David Petraeus, prompting the evergreen question: Why do people with so much to lose risk it all for sex? Public figures, from former Congressman Anthony Weiner to action star and former California Governor Arnold Schwarzenegger, have admitted to straying from their marital vows Petraeus was not the first high-ranking military man to have an affair. World War II general George Patton had an affair with his wife's step-niece. General Douglas MacArthur had a mistress named Isabel Rosario Cooper, whom he met in the Philippines

Leaders like Petraeus tend to be bold risk-takers, a personality trait that is very helpful when leading soldiers into battle. The same trait may make these leaders more likely to take risks in their personal lives, as well. Police officers also fit the profile of risk takers so it should not be all that surprising that academy instructors would put their careers and marriages on the line to further the evolutionary drive to copulate. The human race has had thousands of years of problems with monogamy, and the Police Academy was certainly not immune to the problem.

Recruit police officers were required to follow all the rules and regulations of the police department, but they were also held accountable for rules and policies for recruits while assigned to the Police Academy. Gum chewing, eating on the street, a toothpick in the mouth, long hair, a crooked cap, no name tag, carrying a paper bag or newspaper, entering a bar, or consuming an alcoholic beverage anytime or anywhere, were all recruit violations. By far, however, the mortal sin of recruit misconduct was fraternization.

Socializing between the recruits and the instructors – both in and outside the academy – was forbidden. In fact, all the student officers signed a document acknowledging that they knew and accepted that all fraternization with instructors was forbidden and could result in termination. If a student officer so much as saw an instructor at a restaurant, the recruit was to either avoid talking to the instructor or leave the restaurant. During the MOI course it was drilled into the new instructors that the quickest way back to a patrol command was to develop a personal relationship with a recruit officer.

Recruits were directed to supply four small, passport size photos of themselves on the first day of class. These photos were for the instructors in each discipline. One of the administrative duties I performed on that first day was to hand out blank index cards and instruct the recruits to write their personnel information on the cards, including name, address, phone number, education, and prior occupation. I passed around a stapler and directed the recruits to attach their photo to the top, left corner of the index card.

To this day, I'm not completely sure what the formal purpose of the photo was. It was probably to give the instructor a quick reference of who a recruit was, especially during the early days of the class. I found out very quickly, however, what the informal purpose of the photos were. Rewind to my trip to the subbasement for my first class. It was during that initial meeting with my company that I collected the index cards with the photos attached. I wrapped the stack of index cards in a rubber band and stuffed them in my pocket. After the class I made my way from the subterranean depths of the building to the sixth-floor police science office. I had made it through my first class as an academy instructor intact, and I planned on decompressing for a few minutes at my desk. No sooner did I get seated then I was set upon by four police science instructors – all with the same request. They wanted to see my index cards. I had no idea what they wanted, but I gladly flipped the bound stack of cards onto my desk top. They were all over them, like baseball card collectors looking for a Mickey Mantle card. Finally, I recognized the pattern developing. The male recruit cards were being discarded on my desk, but the five female recruits were obviously the Mickey Mantles of the batch. The female cards were passed around to comments like "She's pretty," and "Great lips." The best comment was reserved for Frank, the instructor with the most time on the job and the longest tenure as an instructor. Frank displayed one of the female cards to the group and tapped his index finger on the photo. "She will be my blow job from this class!" As other instructors entered the office after their initial classes the scene with the index cards repeated itself. The only thing more outrageous would have been if the sergeant who spoke so eloquently during the MOI class about ethics and the evils of fraternization, had burst into the office to join in the drooling over the photos.

Fraternization – the greatest evil defined at the Police Academy – was actually running rampant. The idea of a married male instructor fraternizing with a female recruit was a moral and ethical dilemma in itself, but I wondered why would unmarried instructors risk serious career damage for a tryst with a recruit. The existence of fraternization should not have been a huge surprise. The concept was as old as recorded history. Men can become blind to risk at the sight of an attractive woman, and from an evolutionary perspective, cheating can be a positive mechanism for ensuring gene survival, regardless of risk, scientists say. Wars have been fought and kingdoms lost over women. So, I suppose it shouldn't be all that surprising that some Police Academy instructors would risk their positions for a woman.

One such risk-taker was Police Officer Alex. Alex could best be described as one of those quirky guys you run into once in a while. He was basically a nice guy, and a competent instructor – he was just an odd duck. Alex was odd both in personality and physical appearance. He was short, thin and bald. The shape of his head and nose made him appear very mole-like – not an especially attractive look. Alex also had a quirky love for basketball, and he fancied himself a superior player on the court. Basketball was a serious topic at the Police Academy. Whenever there were no physical training classes taking place in the gym, instructional staff would partake in some really intense games. Alex's size, lack of real skills, and demeanor prevented him from being included in the "Big" games, yet, he insisted with his mantra that he was the best basketball player at the academy and that no one could beat him in a one-on-one game. For some reason, Alex latched onto me as a target to prove his round ball mastery, as he would constantly challenge me to a one-on-one contest. At first, I just laughed off his taunts. I had played ball in school and at 5'11" I was still in reasonably good condition, and while nowhere near the best player on staff, I could give a good account of myself in the big games. There finally reached a point, however, where just to get Alex to leave me alone I gave in and agreed to meet him on-on-one.

Our contest was one of the more bizarre experiences I had at the academy. Alex was left-handed and every time he had the ball he would begin to dribble in a clockwise circle from the top of the key to under the basket and then back to the top of the key. Alex made this circle non-stop for at least five minutes – I'm not exaggerating – five minutes of running in a circle. At first, I covered him closely but eventually I just stopped and stood in the paint scratching my head while I watched this lunatic dribble in a circle with his head down. Finally, when he realized I was no longer interested in covering him he would take an unchallenged layup. The problem for Alex was that even an unchallenged layup was not a certainty, and he missed several of these easy shots. I would get the ball, retreat behind the foul line and take a jump shot. Some shots I made and some I missed. When I missed a shot, Alex would grab the rebound and begin his circular run again. This game was now dragging on for over thirty minutes with the action primarily consisting of me standing with hands on hips watching Alex dribble in his insane circle. Finally, I had to quit because I needed time to shower and change before my scheduled class. Alex threw his arms in the air and declared victory. Who knows, maybe that was his plan all along – to run out the clock on me to where I would be forced to quit. All I knew was that standing on that court while that maniac dribbled around and around me was very strange.

Alex was a law instructor, and a very good one at that. The best academic instructors were usually not assigned recruit companies. The cream of the crop were usually assigned as tutors. Instead of teaching companies, the tutors were assigned to periods during the tour where they instructed voluntary tutoring sessions for recruits who wished extra help with their academic subjects.

Alex was assigned as the law tutor, so several times during the tour he would set up shop in a classroom so recruits could receive extra law help before or after their shift, or during their meal periods. Alex knew the law and he was an outstanding instructor in his ability to reach the recruits. His problem, however, was his ability to reach a little too far to the female recruits. Alex had business cards made that he would issue exclusively to female recruits with instructions to feel free to call him for individual attention. Alex was married and these were days before cell phones, so I don't know what phone number he had on his cards, but he was giving them out to every female recruit who attended a tutoring session.

Alex handed out his cards for at least a year, and I have no knowledge of the results he received. Miraculously, he never got in trouble from his cards. One would think that at least one of his female pupils would have been offended or frightened by his tactics and turned the card over to another instructor or an integrity sergeant. Alex and his cards seemed to be living a charmed life.

There are limits to everything, however, and Alex's luck reached its limit in a big way.

According to academy folklore, Alex received a call from a female recruit who had his card and made an appointment for private tutoring at her apartment – at least that was Alex's story. Whatever the real story was, Alex ended up at the recruit's apartment in Queens on a Saturday night. The recruit lived on the second floor of a building that had an old-style fire escape and somehow, Alex found his way up the fire escape and was attempting to get through the recruit's apartment window. Apparently, this wasn't the type of tutoring the recruit had envisioned so she called the police.

I do give Alex credit for talking himself out of being arrested. According to legend, Alex told the responding officers that he had called the recruit's apartment several times but received no answer. He said that from the sidewalk, he thought he saw a struggle taking place inside the apartment so he quickly climbed the fire escape in an attempt to come to the aid of someone under attack. Whether they bought it or not, no cop wants to arrest another cop, and the female recruit simply did not want to get into trouble herself, so no arrest was made. Alex, however, was done as a tutor, instructor, or anything to do with the Police Academy. His rubber band snapped and would never be repaired again.

Another fraternization extravaganza took out three instructors in one shot. Richie and Bill were physical training instructors while John was assigned to the police science department. As I mentioned previously, recruits and instructors were not permitted to co-mingle in any social setting, but there was one circumstance where the Police Academy command structure would look the other way – at least unofficially.

A signal 10-13 was the radio code for a police officer calling for assistance due to an emergency. It was the most serious call a cop could hear over the radio. A 10-13 was also the name given to a fundraising event for a police officer in need, usually as way to collect funds for exorbitant medical or legal bills, or to provide financial support for the family of a deceased member of the service. For a 10-13 event taking place near the Police Academy, if recruits expressed an interest in attending to contribute to a good cause, there was usually at least tacit approval given. Even though 10-13s were fundraisers for very good causes, let's not lose sight of the fact that the affairs involved social mingling with alcohol being consumed. The 10-13 attended by Richie, Bill, and John was on a Friday night at a bar a couple of blocks from the Police Academy. Male academy instructors plus female recruits plus alcohol equaled big trouble as far as fraternization was concerned.

The 13th Precinct was located on East 21st Street, and was actually connected to the Police Academy building. On Saturday morning the 13th Precinct was quiet. At 8:15 AM a smallish, older man with a bald head and stooped posture approached the desk lieutenant. He was carrying something in his hand that he dropped on the desk. The NYPD identification card belonged to a very pretty female named Stephanie. The tired looking old man was the overnight manager of the small, cheap hotel a block away. He had found the ID card in the bathtub of one of his rooms, and was performing his civic duty by turning it in to a police facility.

It took a minimum of investigation to discover that Stephanie was a recruit officer assigned to the current class at the Police Academy. The ID card was turned over to the Police Academy Integrity & Discipline Unit. On Monday morning, most likely after a sleepless weekend, recruit officer Stephanie was summoned to the Integrity & Discipline office to explain how her ID card found its way into the bathtub of a local hotel.

Recruit officers are inexperienced at all aspects of police work, including "having a story." I knew cops who at the spur of the moment could have concocted a story for that ID card finding its way into that tub that would have brought a sergeant to tears. Possibly a call was received from a sick grandmother who lived near the academy, and the recruit wanted to stay in Manhattan Friday night in case there was an emergency with the grandmother. I know that honesty is the best policy, but frankly, anything would have worked better than the truthful story Stephanie told.

Threatened with immediate termination, Stephanie readily admitted to attending the 10-13 event on Friday evening with two other females from her company. She said that at some point during the evening they began socializing with instructors John, Richie, and Bill. Later that evening, after a great deal of alcohol consumption,

Stephanie said that she and her two classmates found themselves in the local hotel room with Richie, John, and Bill. Stephanie volunteered that her ID card was likely lost during a group sex session in the bathtub.

Stephanie and her two classmates kept their jobs, but like Alex, Richie, Bill and John immediately joined the ranks of ex-instructors as they found themselves transferred out of the Police Academy that same day.

Some of the problems male instructors experienced with female recruits had less to do with fraternization and more to do with stupidity. Such was the case for Police Officer John, an instructor in the social science department.

Life is too short to spend mired in feuds and vindictiveness. This may be easy for me to say because I have always had the ability to get along with others. I never had a problem working with people, even those people I did not care for. As a matter of fact, during my ever- lengthening life span, there is only one person I can think of who I disliked to the point that I actually wished him bad fortune - John. I mentioned police officer John in another Dark Knights book, and without getting into the sordid details of my distaste for this man I will just say that John was already a recruit instructor at the Police Academy when I arrived for my first class.

Naturally, recruits were required to be in uniform at the academy, but they were also required to travel to and from the academy in uniform. There were no locker room facilities for recruits to change in or out of uniform. at the beginning and end of their tours of duty. There were times, however, when a blind eye would be turned toward the issue of recruits changing into civilian clothing at the end of their tour, such as when receiving the tacit approval to attend an aforementioned 10-13 event. For these events, recruits would unofficially be permitted to change into civilian clothes at the end of a day tour so they could attend and contribute to the good cause.

  Recruit officer Maria had decided to attend a 10-13 function after a day tour. When her tour ended she took her academy bag containing her civilian clothes and changed in the fifth-floor ladies room. Maria was assigned to one of John's companies, so it was with a degree of surprise that he encountered Maria wearing civilian clothing in the stairway. John questioned why she was out of uniform and Maria explained she was told she could change clothes to attend the 10-13 event. One of the many reasons I disliked John was the arrogant manner in which he would regularly make smart-ass remarks. Therefore, once John realized Maria was authorized to be in civilian clothing, he could not just let her go. His nature called for a smart-ass remark. In this case, the remark bit him in the ass when he commented. "I hope you wore clean underwear."

  We can debate how damning a statement that was, and I try to be objective by masking my hatred for John. Regardless of how you feel about the statement, Maria didn't appreciate it one bit, and she immediately went to the Integrity and Disciple office and reported the comment to a sergeant. John got formally written up for the comment, but that wasn't the best part. John had to apologize to Maria in front of the entire recruit company. I would have paid to have been in that classroom during the apology. Sometimes there is justice in the world.

Despite my personal feelings toward John, I realize he made a stupid statement with no malice intended. I made such an innocent, yet stupid statement to a female recruit during my first class that caused me to lose sleep for two nights.

About a month into my first police science class I gave out a quiz to my company during the last portion of the class. My quizzes were usually twenty fill-in or multiple choice questions, so it only took about fifteen minutes to complete a quiz. As the recruits finished their quiz, I would allow them to leave the classroom and take a break for few extra minutes before their next scheduled class.

I sat at my desk in the front of the classroom collecting quizzes one by one. Sitting in the first seat directly in front of my desk was recruit office Joanne. As Joanne concentrated on her quiz, I could not help but notice something odd about her attire. Recruit officers, just like uniformed officers on patrol, were required to wear black socks as part of their uniform. Being in uniform was important at all times during a police officer's career, but it was an extremely sensitive topic for a recruit at the Police Academy. While Joanne continued to work on her quiz, my attention was drawn to her, specifically to the area near her shoes. The contrast made by the white socks between her dark blue uniform pants and highly shined black shoes was like a neon sign screaming – look at me! I couldn't believe this. This recruit was advertising her white socks right in front of me.

During orientation, the recruits were issued two Student Training Activity Report Cards (Star Cards), which they had to carry in their uniform shirt pocket at all times while at the Police Academy. If there was a minor violation or problem, such as a student not doing homework, forgetting a uniform item, or wearing white socks, instructors would take a star card, and the deficiency would be noted on the recruit's final evaluation. Seven pulled star cards or a more serious infraction of the rules would result in a Command Discipline (CD), a formal disciplinary process that could result in termination.

During my first class I was hesitant to pull star cards. I was a cop – not a supervisor – and I was still having trouble accepting that I was, in fact, a supervisor for these recruits. I was reluctant to initiate any formal discipline against another cop (even a recruit) when I could handle the situation informally myself. Such was my intent with recruit officer Joanne. She was wearing those white socks right in front of me and I had to call her out on it, even if I wasn't going to pull a star card.

Joanne was the last recruit in the company to finish the quiz, so my reinstruction session would be easy since it was only Joanne and myself in the classroom. She dropped the quiz on my desk and turned to retrieve her recruit bag. Before Joanne could make her exit from the classroom I began my reinstruction session. "Officer, I don't ever want to see those white socks again."

Joanne lowered her head contritely. "I'm sorry sir."

I continued, "I should take a star card from you, but I'm not."

"Thank you, sir. It won't happen again." Joanne picked up her bag and began her move to the door.

I wanted her to know that just because I didn't take a star card, it didn't mean that other instructors during the remainder of the tour weren't going to pull a card. "Officer, you're going to interact with a lot of instructors during the rest of the tour."

Then, I said it. "Officer, if I were you I would pull my pants down right now."

Obviously, my intent was to recommend that she hide the white socks as best as she could by keeping her pants lower, but I realized immediately how my words could be taken. For a moment, Joanne and I simply stared at each other, looking equally fearful. I considered trying to explain that I really didn't mean for her to actually take her pants off, but I knew that a rambling attempt at an explanation would only make matters worse.

I spent the next few days waiting for the call to the Integrity & Discipline office that would expedite my return to patrol. The call never came. Nevertheless, the incident taught me a very valuable lesson for the academy, the rest of my time on the job, and for life – think before you speak.

CHAPTER 5: THE PANAMA LOTTERY COMES TO POLICE SCIENCE

Looking back, for a transit cop used to patrolling subway stations in the heat of New York City's blistering summers and the frigid cold days of winter, assignment to the New York City Police Academy was the greatest thing since the invention of yoga pants. The first six- month class was intense with all the curriculum preparation required, but once I had the lesson plans, the atmosphere changed drastically.

The typical day required me to teach two classes for a total of three hours in front of the recruits. That was it! The rest of the day or night was mine. I could work out in the mini-gym, play basketball or racquetball when the gym was available, run next to the FDR Drive, or just sit in the instructor lounge and watch TV. Like myself, all the transit instructors detailed to the NYPD academy realized what a sweet deal they had. I could never understand the negative attitude many of the NYPD instructors had regarding the academy, especially those instructors with very little time on the job. Some of them would constantly whine if they had to cover an additional class and work 4.5 hours instead of three hours during a tour.

One of the biggest NYPD whiners was a cop named Norman. Besides being an all-star whiner, Norman was a very nice guy and also a very excitable guy. Norman had seven years on the job and had been at the academy for three years. He was of Panamanian descent and was very tall and lean. When Norman became excited, which was a daily occurrence, he spoke very fast and became difficult to understand with his thick accent.

Norman told the same story to everyone who would listen – instructors, sergeants, lieutenants, even recruits. Norman related how he would never stay with the NYPD for twenty years because he planned on being wealthy long before that time and settling in a mansion in his native Panama. Norman would explain that his wealth accumulation plan involved the Panamanian lottery. He said that the odds in that lottery were far better than any lottery in America and that it was just a matter of time before he hit big. In the meantime, Norman continued to buy his lottery tickets every week and to whine and complain about every aspect of academy life.

In general, cops tend to possess a universal skill set. Cops are usually skilled at talking to people, resolving conflict, and functioning well in stressful situations. Additionally, most cops are expert ball breakers, with some possessing elite credentials. Doug was one of those elite ball breakers who could very quickly and effectively run an elaborate scam for the sole purpose of breaking someone's balls. Norman, and his frequent Panamanian lottery rants was the perfect target for Doug.

One of Norman's frequent lines was that he would be gone from the NYPD and the country the moment he was notified he had hit the lottery. As such, he regularly volunteered the fact that he listed the phone at his desk in the police science office as one of the methods for the Panamanian lottery officials to contact him. One late morning during a day tour, Norman was holding court in the police science office, conducting a particularly animated rant about how he could sense his ship was coming in soon, and that it was only a matter of time before he hit the Panamanian lottery. Doug was seated at his desk on the other side of the office, and I could almost see the light bulb illuminate over Doug's head. As Norman continued his emotional speech to a couple of nearby instructors, Doug quietly left the police science office. He didn't go to class, the men's room, the gym, or the library. Doug walked about twenty feet down the hall and entered the phone booth recessed into the wall. (Remember, these were days before cell phones and caller IDs). A few seconds after Doug left the office, Norman's diatribe was interrupted by his desk phone. His eyes were as wide as saucers as he excitedly wrote some information on a notepad. Norman hung up the phone and let out a blood curdling scream that resulted in personnel from other offices on the sixth floor running into the hallway to see what was happening. No one in the police science office knew what happened because after his howl, Norman bolted from the office and was last seen sprinting west on 20th Street.

    No one knew what had happened or what to do. Should we go after him? Should we call the local precinct to look for him? Doug walked back into the police science office and shed some light on the situation. "I know what happened," he stated with a wry grin. All activity stopped as all eyes were fixed on Doug. "He won the Panamanian Lottery."

"How do you know?" Alex responded. "You weren't even here."

With his grin becoming wider, Doug said, "I called him."

There was that brief moment of silence when everyone considered what a horrible thing this was to do to Norman, but the feeling of conscience and silence quickly gave way to hilarity. This had to be one of the greatest pranks I had ever seen pulled off, and it got better when Doug pridefully explained the details. He related that he had just called Norman from the phone booth representing himself as someone from a law firm located at the World Trade Center. He said that his firm was the United States agent for the Panamanian lottery, and that Norman had won $2.5 million. Doug told Norman that all he had to do was come to the law office on the 82nd floor within thirty days to claim his winnings. Being an expert ballbreaker, Doug realized there was a good chance for a part two of this prank, so he gave Norman the phone booth number as his office number. This number wouldn't raise Norman's suspicions because the phone booth had a different exchange then the academy office phone numbers, and it had the normal Manhattan 212 area code.

About thirsty minutes after Norman fled the scene, Doug went back to the scene of his crime and sat in the phone booth. It only took five minutes for the phone to ring. If he didn't know what the call was about, Doug never would have been able to understand Norman, but since he knew what was taking place, it was easy for him to calmly state, "I'm sorry, sir. you're in the wrong tower. My office is on the 82nd floor in the other tower."

With that, Doug ended the prank from his end. There wasn't much more he could do, short of telling Norman that he had to go to the airport and catch the next flight to Panama. Believe me, I'm sure he at least momentarily considered that. Doug wasn't completely heartless. He actually went and covered Norman's class so he wouldn't get in trouble for abandoning his recruits. About an hour later, Norman entered the police science office and sat at his desk. There was fire in his eyes. He wanted a fight, but he didn't know who to initiate conflict with. He was waiting for someone to laugh or take credit for the elaborate hoax, but no one said a word to him. The office was business as usual. Doug put the final touch on the episode when he entered the office after covering Norman's class. "Hey, what happened to you?" he said to Norman. Before Norman could answer, Doug continued. "Don't worry. I covered your class. The sergeant didn't even realize you were gone."

Norman slumped in his chair, completely deflated. "Thanks," he mumbled.

CHAPTER 6: HIGHWAY

Before the merger with the NYPD, there wasn't much variety in the life of a transit cop. Northbound/southbound is what transit cops called the job of uniformed subway foot patrol. Each transit district normally only had two patrol vehicles, so the chances of patrolling in a car were very limited. To be fair, the Transit Police Department did have some specialized units. Within each command were plainclothes anti-crime units. There was also a Detective Division, K9 Unit, and Emergency Medical Rescue Unit. For most transit cops, however, the world consisted of northbound/southbound. That is why I thought I had died and gone to heaven when I was detailed to the NYPD Police Academy as an instructor. The academy was one of the very few opportunities to be detailed to an NYPD operation. As a matter of fact, the only other unit I knew of where transit cops were detailed to the NYPD was the Applicant Investigation Unit, where transit cops worked side by side with NYPD officers in investigating applicants seeking to be hired as police officers.

The NYPD was filled with specialized units that transit cops could not access. In the NYPD, cops could aspire to work in the mounted unit, highway unit, aviation, and harbor, just to name a few. Transit had no boats, aircraft, or horses, although there was an infamous shirt that paid tribute to the Transit Police Mounted Unit. On the front of the shirt was a picture of a uniformed cop riding atop a huge rat. Under the illustration were the bold words TRANSIT

POLICE MOUNTED UNIT. Some of the rats I saw late at night in the subway were of the size where I might have been able to saddle them.

Police Officer Eddie was a transit cop assigned to the police science department. Eddie had been an instructor for a while. In fact, he was part of the transit police instructional staff five years earlier when I went through the Transit Police Academy on 155th Street. Eddie was a character. As recruits, we feared his disciplinary style of instruction, and five years later I smiled to see that the current recruits still feared Eddie. Eddie was extremely outspoken with his peers and his bosses. He was a member of the Blue Knights motorcycle club, and would routinely come to the academy wearing his Blue Knights jacket. Even though the Blue Knights was a club for law enforcement officers, an NYPD lieutenant told Eddie that it was not professional for the recruits to see him coming and going from the academy in the outfit of a motorcycle gang. Eddie responded by enhancing his attire to include a black leather jacket with metal studs with a helmet similar to the style worn by the German Army in World War II.

Eddie loved his motorcycle and would talk non-stop about his desire to work as a motorcycle cop in a highway district. I always found his passion odd, because as a transit cop he had as much chance to work on a motorcycle, as he did on a boat or aircraft. As an aside, however, I must mention that the most industrious transit cop I ever knew actually got himself put in charge of a one-man Transit Police Aviation Unit. This cop was one of my instructors at 155th Street, and he had been a helicopter pilot in the Army. He was actually able to convince Transit Police management that it would be a good idea to maintain aerial surveillance over the large train yards spread throughout the city. The Department agreed, so every day, this cop would drive to an airport on Long Island (by the way, he lived on Long Island) and fly a helicopter around the city's train yards. He would then fly back to the airport on Long Island and go home. Ingenious! Now, back to Eddie.

During my initial two-year tour as an instructor, the Police Academy won the unit citation as the best specialized unit for the year. The Commanding Officer of the Police Academy (called COPA) called the entire academy staff into the auditorium to express his thanks for a job well done. This Deputy Chief was so happy about receiving the award, he offered to help anyone from the instructional staff to move to any unit they desired. There was silence in the auditorium until Eddie called out "I'd like to go to highway."

The chief shrugged and said, "That shouldn't be too hard."

There was chuckling throughout the auditorium as most instructors realized who had made the request. A lieutenant trotted up on stage and whispered in the chief's ear. The chief chuckled and said, "Some things, like getting a transit cop into highway, are beyond my control."

Eddie simply shrugged and responded. "Thanks anyway, Chief. It never hurts to ask."

The merger of the Transit Police into the NYPD occurred eight years later, but Eddie was already retired, so he never got to revisit his dream of being a motorcycle cop. As a matter of fact, there was a rather weird ending to Eddie's saga on the job that I mentioned in another volume of Dark Knights, but for continuity's sake, I think it is worth repeating.

When I arrived at the NYPD academy, Eddie had a little over fourteen years on the job. At that time, twenty years qualified a police officer for a full half pay pension, but a cop could vest at fifteen years and retire with a lesser pension. Eddie had fallen in love with a town somewhere in Virginia and had bought a home there. He moved his wife and kids to the home in Virginia even though he still had almost a year to go before he could vest out. During that time the academy was running with weekends off, so Eddie would drive to Virginia on the weekends and spend the week in New York City. Eddie didn't want to waste money on an apartment or room, so he simply lived in the Police Academy. He slept in the instructor's lounge and showered in the locker room. After going through all this hardship to make it to Virginia, I found out that Eddie got divorced, and his wife and kids stayed in Virginia while he remained in New York.

In an equally bizarre twist, several years ago, one of the secretaries at my office turned out to be Eddie's second wife. When he finally retired, Eddie became the caretaker for a cemetery, and he and Iris lived in a house on the cemetery grounds. Iris said that one day – Eddie was gone. She elaborated that Eddie had been able to buy a house in Florida and give notice of his resignation from the cemetery job without her knowing. One day, Eddie and all his belongings were gone, and the manager of the cemetery told her a new caretaker would be moving in to the house the next day.

CHAPTER 7: YOU WANT TO STEP OUTSIDE?

It did not take long for Police Academy instructors to obtain veteran status. There were always some new instructors coming on board at the beginning of every class, so even an instructor with only one class under his or her belt could be a valuable source of advice and counsel for a newbie instructor.

When I began my second six-month academy class, I found myself approached for advice by a new instructor with a very unique problem. As I began my second cycle at the academy I had a little more than five and a half years on the job and I was about to turn thirty. I was still young and far from being a grizzled veteran, but I had some time on the job and I was older than the recruits. I make this point because it plays prominently into the issue regarding Police Officer John. John had joined the NYPD at the minimum age of twenty, and with just over three years on the job, he was now an instructor at the ripe old age of twenty-three. John was physically small with a baby face that would have made no one question that he may still be in high school.

During the first few weeks after John had been assigned to the police science department, he wasn't exactly winning friends and allies. John was very self-confident, but most of the police science staff described the personality of this twenty-three- year old as arrogant. He just seemed to have an awful lot to say for a young kid who was brand new at the academy.

I don't know whether this is a positive or negative quality, but I have always had the ability to get along with just about anyone. As a matter of fact, there is only one person I can think of who I despised to the point that I could not think about maintaining social pleasantries. This person happened to be an academy instructor who I previously mentioned in a chapter of this book.

I certainly had not become great friends with John, but as we entered the third week of classes he was astute enough to realize that I was probably the only instructor in the office who would listen to his troubles. I was sitting at my desk going over a lesson plan when my concentration was interrupted by a tap on the shoulder. "Can I talk to you in the hall?"

I knew immediately by the look on John's face that something was wrong. He had that faraway look in his eyes that I had seen many times in victims of some physical or emotional trauma. John was present in body, but his mind was far away.

"What's up Johnny?"

John was lacking his usual self-confidence as he stammered in an attempt to find the right words. "How do you handle it when a recruit challenges you?"

"I keep it simple, Johnny. If they don't do the work, I talk to them and tell them that they aren't hurting me, they are only hurting themselves." I smiled. "Remember, it's not personal. If they fail out of the academy it's their career that is ruined, not yours."

My advice did not seem to change John's troubled expression one bit. He shook his head. "No, I mean what do you do if a recruit physically challenges you?"

"What?" I was confused. "You mean like challenges you to a fight?"

John nodded, his eyes still miles away. I took a deep breath and put my hand on John's shoulder. "What happened?"

John said that during the first two weeks of the class there was one recruit in his company who was a constant problem. He said that this recruit was constantly talking during class, and making snide remarks under his breath. John stated that during the police science class thirty minutes earlier, this same recruit made another remark loud enough to prompt the entire class to laugh. This outburst prompted John to direct the offensive recruit to the hall so he could talk to him privately. He said that once they were in the hall, he laid down the law by telling the recruit that his behavior and attitude was unacceptable, and that the recruit responded by telling John that he was going to meet him after class and beat the shit out of him.

"What?" I was stunned.

"That's right," John nodded

The short time I had known John caused me to consider that he probably didn't actually tell the recruit that his behavior and attitude was unacceptable. John's statement had probably been closer to the recruit's threat to beat the shit out of him. Nonetheless, recruits waiting outside the academy to beat up instructors was completely unacceptable. Now that the story was over, John was expecting some advice. Unfortunately, I didn't feel the wisdom of Solomon oozing out of me. Frankly, I felt like saying, "good luck. I hope things turn out well for you," before returning to my lesson plan. As much as I would have liked to, I knew I couldn't ignore the problem. John had sought my advice, and I felt I owed him something, so I stated the obvious. I told him that the one hundred percent wrong path would be to fight the recruit after class. I emphasized that there were a variety of possible outcomes from a fight – all bad. It was possible for John, the recruit, or both of them to be arrested for fighting in the street. Additionally, John would instantly be transferred back to patrol and the recruit would immediately be fired if the fight became known.

I took a deep breath. "Let me see his index card."

John disappeared into the police science office and returned a few seconds later holding a stack of index cards bound by a rubber band. He removed the rubber band and flipped through the cards. "Here," he stated as he offered a card.

The recruit's name was Joseph and he lived in Bensonhurst, Brooklyn. He was twenty-seven years old, which I thought may be part of the problem, seeing that John was only twenty-three.

"Where is the company now?" I inquired

"In law – room 502."

I shook my head. "You can't just let this go, Johnny, but if you report it, the kid will be fired with one hundred percent certainty."

John stared silently at me, apparently waiting for me to suggest an alternate solution. I tapped the index card against my knuckles. "Let me talk to the kid before you do anything."

"OK by me." John seemed relieved that I was going to take some action.

As I walked down the hall toward 502, the reality of what I could be getting myself into began to set in. First of all, I had not really formulated a plan of what I was going say to the recruit, and second, what was I going to do if this kid told me that I would get an ass kicking as soon as he was done with John? Oh well. As I tapped on the glass window of the door to Room 502 I realized that there was no turning back now.

Police Officer Tommy opened the door. "What's up?"

"I glanced at the index card to refresh my knowledge of the name. "I need to see recruit Joe for a minute."

"Sure, "Tommy responded. He closed the door and a moment later it re-opened. I was momentarily stunned. The index card did not reflect that Joe was 6' 5" tall and at least 250 pounds. As this behemoth stood at attention before me I observed a complex look on his face. He surmised why I wanted to talk to him and there was definitely anger in his eyes. There was also a look of fear on his face, as he had obviously considered that his macho act had the potential for getting him into serious trouble.

I still wasn't quite sure what I wanted to say, but at this point I knew I had to say something, and I hoped the right words would emerge. "I'm going to make this quick, officer. One of the first things you learn on patrol is that you cannot allow someone to take advantage of you and disrespect you. Even if you don't care about how you look, letting someone get away with that type of behavior only emboldens them and makes them more dangerous during their next encounter with a cop. You can understand that, right?"

Recruit Joe remained at attention and stared straight ahead. "Yes, sir."

"So," I continued, "I know you can also understand that a Police Academy instructor cannot ignore threats from recruits, nor can they meet them outside after work to settle their differences."

Joe repeated a very low "Yes sir."

"How important is it for you to be a cop?" I asked

"It's everything to me," Joe responded. "My grandfather was a cop and my father was a cop. All I ever wanted to be was a cop."

"That's great," I said. "But I hope you realize that when instructor John goes to the lieutenant in the Recruit Administration office and reports this incident, you will be processed for termination today."

Joe remained at the position of attention, but his body seemed to slightly deflate. Additionally, I noticed his bottom lip quivering and his eyes began to moisten. "Stand at ease, officer," I said. "Follow me,"

I walked down the hall toward the stairway. I knew there were no recruit companies on meal period at this time, so I led Joe into the empty third floor recruit cafeteria. "I need a drink," I commented as I scanned the soda machine until my finger found the Diet Coke button. "You want something?" I asked as I removed my can from the machine.

"No thank you, sir."

I sat at the end of one of the long cafeteria tables and motioned for Joe to have a seat opposite me. I took the first sip of my soda before continuing the business at hand. "So, what actually happened between you and your instructor?"

Joe looked down at the table while he shook his head and bit his lip. "I was just acting like a moron in class, and the instructor called me out on it. I would have done the same thing."

I put my soda can on the table. "Then why did you threaten to kick his ass?"

Joe shrugged. "It was just a stupid street reflex. You know – where I grew up in Brooklyn, someone threatens to kick the shit out of you – you threaten to kick the shit out of them. It's just the law of the street. I know I was way out of line but my instincts took over."

I put up my hand in the universal sign for stop. "Wait a minute. Are you telling me that your instructor threatened you first?"

Joe shrugged again. "Yeah," he calmly answered. "He said if I acted up once more in class he was going to take me outside and whip my ass."

The entire picture was becoming clear. Joe was still dead wrong to challenge John, but in my mind the whole flavor of the incident changed knowing that John had been the first party to threaten fisticuffs.

I took the final sip of my soda before flipping the can in the recyclable trash bin. I reached over and slapped Joe's forearm. "Here's what I think, Joe. I think that if I bring you upstairs to the police science office right now, and you apologize to Instructor John, then you will have a long and rewarding career with the NYPD, provided you behave yourself for your remaining time at the academy."

Joe's face lit up like a candle. "Thank you so much, sir."

Two minutes later I directed Joe to stand at parade rest outside the police science office door. John was seated at his desk, but he immediately shot to his feet when he saw me enter the office.

"How did it go?" he asked.

"Well," I replied, "your recruit is outside the office waiting to apologize to you."

"Do you think that's a good idea?" John asked.

"What do you mean?"

"I mean, he physically threatens me and then says he's sorry, so now I'm supposed to forget the whole thing."

The annoyance in my tone was palpable. "You do what you think is right, Johnny, but seeing as you threatened to kick his ass first – yeah, I think it's in everyone's best interests to accept his apology and move on."

John stood for a moment in silence nodding his head slightly. Finally, he began walking toward the office door. "You know, I think it would be a good idea for me to accept his apology. I don't really want to get the kid fired."

That was it. No thanks for your help – that was great advice – nothing. I could see why John had become so popular with the rest of the staff in such a short time.

CHAPTER 8: EVALUATIONS

As great as Police Academy life was for an instructor, it wasn't without controls. All instructors, particularly the new instructors were observed and evaluated on a regular basis by sergeants from their academic discipline. Sgt. Sean was one of my police science squad sergeants who sat in on my classes regularly. Sean was also detailed to the academy from the Transit Police Department and he was a very good guy. Sean was also something of a character.

One of Sean's most endearing qualities was that he was basically a street guy who fancied himself an academic elite. That unique combination resulted in "Slip" as a nickname for Sean. Even during the mid-1980s the nickname was somewhat obsolete, but today the moniker is downright antiquated. Slip referred to a character in the old TV comedy series "The Bowery Boys." Slip Mahoney was the leader of the gang, and part of the regular comedy routine was that Slip was constantly trying to prove his intellectual superiority by using big words, or in his case - misusing big words. The same principle applied to Sean. He routinely tried to display his advanced intellect through his advanced vocabulary, both verbally and in writing, but in most instances, he would fall flat on his face through the improper use of the words he was using. The great quality Sean possessed, however, was that he didn't care. He could have just humiliated himself by butchering several words in a sentence and it did not dissuade him from using the same words minutes later.

Sean had special words he liked, and when he latched onto a favorite "high-brow" word, he stayed with it. Sean sat in on my classes at least a dozen times, and somewhere on each evaluation form he wrote, "the instructor utilized the Socratic method of instruction." Every time I sat with Sean to go over the evaluation, part of the script was always the same. Sean would hand me the evaluation, and at some point, while I was reading his comments he would ask if I knew what the Socratic method of instruction was. I would always say no, to give him the satisfaction of enlightening me as to how the Greek philosopher Socrates would lecture groups of people, and how the Socratic method meant that I was lecturing the recruits. Sean's evaluations were always good, so why not let him feel like he was exploiting his intellectual superiority. On one occasion, however, I had to say something to Sean about his evaluation.

Normally, a sergeant would enter the class at the beginning and stay for about fifteen minutes. In this case, however, Sean entered my room when the class started, sat in a chair in the back of the room, but stayed for the entire 90-minute class. It was unusual, but it didn't bother me. I just continued with the class as normal. About 45-minutes into the class I could sense something was going on. The recruits were doing their best to hide it, but many of them were catching glances toward the back of the room and doing their best not to smile. I was at a loss to figure out what was happening, but before I said anything to the recruits, I understood the situation. Sean had lingered in my class for a prolonged period of time for a good reason - he was sound asleep. I didn't want to do anything to embarrass him any more than he already was, so I just pressed on with the class and let him sleep. When I dismissed the class, I hoped that the noise from the recruits vacating their desks would wake him, and it did. As usual, it was virtually impossible to embarrass Sean. He yawned and left the classroom behind the recruits without a word. Later that day, it was time for me to sit with Sean to go over my evaluation. As usual he had written his piece about the Socratic method of instruction, but he also wrote that I needed to interject more overhead questions during the class. I was momentarily stunned. I was looking at a criticism of my class written by a sergeant who had been asleep during the entire class time. I was about to challenge Sean on this critique, when a big dose of sanity came over me. Why would I fight it? The evaluation was still good. All I would succeed in doing was pissing off a sergeant who could return to my class the next day and really stick it to me. Instead, I sat and listened to Sean talk about Socrates again.

CHAPTER 9: WORKING OUT

When I arrived at the NYPD Police Academy to begin my tenure as an instructor, the Commanding Officer of the Recruit Training School was Captain A. The only interaction I had with the captain was via his welcome aboard speech to my group of new instructors. He seemed like a nice enough fellow, and he probably was.

One of the many benefits to working at the Police Academy was the use of the facilities, in particular the gym. Every day there were very serious basketball and paddleball games taking place, while grunts and groans resonated from the universal weightlifting machine. Of course, use of the gym by the staff was only possible during periods when recruit physical training classes were not taking place. I soon learned that this rule apparently did not apply to the Commanding Officer of the Recruit Training School.

During my MOI course it was recommended that instructors observe their companies during physical training class every now and then. A recruit's struggles during physical training may help to explain changes in performance in the academic disciplines. There was a small balcony above the gym that could be accessed via the second floor. From this small, dark perch, instructors could watch the workouts in relative anonymity. The first time I watched a physical training class from the balcony I was accompanied by Police Officer Richie. Richie had twelve years on the NYPD and had been an academy instructor for five years. Richie was teaching social science to the same company I had been assigned for police science, and it was Richie's suggestion that we take a look at how our recruits were faring in the gym.

Physical training classes were conducted in two parts. The first part of the class was group calisthenics and a run in company formations around the perimeter of the gym. The second part of the class was a tactical lesson in subjects like handcuffing, baton use, and first aid. At the command of the instructor on the platform, the recruits spread out across the gym floor to prepare for their exercises. The instructor on the platform called the cadence for pushups, sit ups, squat thrusts, and jumping jacks. As I watched the physical exertion on the gym floor, I noticed someone enter the gym. It was Captain A. As usual, the very fit captain was impeccably dressed in his custom fit uniform white shirt. I assumed he had come to see the chairman of the physical training department, but Richie poked my side and said, "Watch this."

The recruits had now mustered in company formations to begin a two-mile run around the perimeter of the gym. The universal machine was stuffed into the northeast corner of the gym, and Captain A. made his way directly to the universal. With no hesitation the captain laid back on the bench and slid into position to perform bench presses. He started out light, but every few minutes he would adjust the pin to add more weight to his lift. I'm not sure how much weight he was pressing, but each rep resulted in a loud grunt as he pushed the weight up. The captain's grunts quickly transitioned to screams as the weight continued to increase. His volume was so loud that almost every recruit was staring over at him with confused looks on their faces as they ran by.

There is absolutely nothing wrong with an intense workout, but remember, the captain was not in work out cloths - he was in full uniform. As he moved from station to station on the machine, I could clearly see that he was in a pool of sweat with his white uniform shirt soaked through with perspiration. When he completed his reps at the final station the captain stretched his arms and departed the gym without even wiping his face with a towel. I looked at Richie and was greeted by a huge grin. "You'll get used to it," he said. "He does this every day. He works out in his uniform until he's swimming in his own sweat, and then he goes back to his office and continues working." Richie shook his head. "That's one hard core dude."

I shook my head. "Maybe his PAA who has to be in his office all day is the hard core one."

CHAPTER 10: A HAPPY VISIT

A trainer is blessed with the opportunity to touch many lives. The Police Academy was my springboard into the world of training. Besides police recruits, I have taught police in-service training classes, police promotional classes, private security guards, defensive driving classes, and I am an adjunct professor at a New York College. As I look back, I have faced thousands of students in the classroom. It is unfortunate that it is impossible to remember the vast majority of my students. To this day I will still have people stop me in the street and mention that I was their instructor in the Police Academy or that I taught their defensive driving class a few years earlier. Of course, there are some students who stand out for both positive and negative reasons. In an upcoming chapter, I will detail the story of two recruits who never made it out of the academy. On the positive side I had two recruits in my companies who attained the rank of deputy chief.

An interesting phenomenon with police recruits was how many of them would come back to visit at the academy after they graduated, usually, within six months after graduation. I was always flattered when a former recruit would stop by to say hello and tell about his first few months on patrol. Sometimes, these new patrol officers would actually come to my classroom, and if I could, I would let them come in and answer questions from the class about life immediately after graduation. Former students visiting in such a manner were usually a very positive experience. There are, however, exceptions to everything.

Chris had been one of those recruits who didn't make much an impression, either positive or negative. He quietly went through his six months of academy training doing all his work and passing all his exams. I liked Chris, but frankly, he was one of the last people I expected to show up at my classroom door after graduation. Nevertheless, there he was. It was about one month until my current class of recruits was to graduate, so my initial reaction upon seeing Chris was very positive, because I was sure the class would have a lot of questions about their post-graduation assignments. I was a little embarrassed because I did not know where Chris had been assigned after graduation, and since he was dressed in civilian attire, I had no collar brass insignia to give me a clue. When I saw Chris standing outside my classroom door I smiled and motioned for him to enter the room. That was my first mistake. As Chris made his entry I introduced him as a former recruit who could give them great insights into life after graduation.

Chris did not wait for any questions. He immediately said, "Let's be careful out there."

While it was a bit strange to just blurt out a statement, I had to admit it was good advice, so I didn't say anything. Again, before a question could be raised, Chris spoke again. "Nanu Nanu."

What? Now I was confused and beginning to become alarmed. But I didn't want to jump the gun with my anxiety as I walked toward Chris. Maybe he had said something very profound and I just didn't understand him. Obviously, my recruit class didn't understand him either, as they sat in stone-faced silence. I reached out and placed my hand on Chris's shoulder. I figured I would provide some guidance for his next statement. "Chris, why don't you tell the class about the schedule in your command right after graduation."

My hand was still on his shoulder when Chris turned toward me and squinted. "What you talkin bout, Willis?"

In that instant, clarity set in. Clarity did not make me feel good but at least I knew what was going on. Chris had been blurting out a series of catch phrases from popular television shows of the time. What I was hoping had been a safety recommendation had actually been the catchphrase from Hill Street Blues – let's be careful out there. When I thought Chris was possibly clearing his throat, he was actually saying the Mork and Mindy catchphrase – nanu nanu. His final statement was not a response to my prompt for information, but was in fact, another catchphrase, this time from the sitcom Different Strokes.

The question now became why would this quiet, cooperative rookie cop who had sat attentively in my classroom several months earlier present himself to my current recruits for the express purpose of blurting out a series of TV catch phrases. As I leaned in to whisper to Chris that he should go, the reason for his behavior became crystal clear. The smell of alcohol on his breath was the only explanation I needed. The glassy look in his eye only reinforced my diagnosis. Chris was drunk. Now I had a real dilemma. Police officers are supposed to be fit for duty at all times, even when off duty. Even though this moron was stupid enough to come into the Police Academy in an intoxicated condition and disrupt my class, I was not going to officially report the incident. Chris was on probation and the consequences for him could be severe - possibly even termination. But I also did not want to throw an intoxicated person out to the sidewalk. For all I knew, Chris had driven to the academy and was going to get back in his car and drive in that impaired condition. Meanwhile, I still had a classroom full of recruits waiting for me. The solution to my problem came in the form of a figure in work-out clothes lumbering down the hall. Andy was a police science instructor who had attended the same MOI course as me. Andy had some free time and was on his way down to the gym for an hour of some intense paddle ball. I really did not want to ruin his plans, but I had little choice. I pleaded with Andy to take the drunken Chris off my hands and to keep him somewhere until my class was over in 45-minutes. Chris reluctantly obliged and departed with his arm draped around Chris's shoulder.

    When my class ended I ran to the police science office to find Andy. He wasn't there. I was pondering my next search location when I observed Andy walk past the police science office, sweat gleaning off his body after several intense paddleball matches. I ran into the hall and threw my arms out to the side. I didn't have to ask the question. Andy knew exactly what I wanted to know. "Just calm down and follow me," he said.

Andy was on his way to the showers in the staff locker room on the sixth floor, but to access the locker room, you had to first enter the instructor's lounge. Andy passed through the lounge door first, and when I stepped inside Andy smiled and pointed to the sofa. Stretched out on the sofa, snoring mightily was Chris. Chris slept for several hours and I didn't see him before he left. In fact, I never saw Chris again. Maybe he was too embarrassed to contact me. All I know is that from that day forward, I developed a whole new philosophy regarding former recruits visiting me at the Police Academy.

CHAPTER 11: THE ROTTEN APPLE

A return roll call was one of the informal disciplinary tools an instructor could use. If something happened during the day that the instructor didn't like, he could direct the company to present themselves for a return roll call. At the end of classes, instead of hurrying to make buses and trains, the company was directed to report to the campus deck in company formation. The instructor could keep the company in formation for up to fifteen minutes. After fifteen minutes, union issues regarding overtime kicked in so fifteen minutes was the cut off.

I wasn't a big fan of the return roll call for a couple of reasons. First, I very rarely became upset enough at the entire company that I wanted to keep them after the tour of duty, and secondly, and more importantly, by inconveniencing the recruits by keeping them after class I was also inconveniencing myself. There are exceptions to everything, however, and I recall one instance where I would have held the company at attention for a return roll call of eight hours if I thought I could have gotten away with it.

The Police Academy building was located at 235 East 20th Street with its entrance being on 20th Street. The entire building occupied the space between 20th and 21st Streets, so the rear of the academy bordered and looked out onto 21st Street. The 13th Precinct was not affiliated in any way to the Police Academy except for the fact that the precinct was located on 21st Street and was actually part of the single structure that was the Police Academy. In fact, there was a door in the academy parking garage that connected to the 13th precinct. Sharing space adjacent to the 13th Precinct was Emergency Service Unit Truck 1. ESU is a component of the Special Operations Bureau. The unit is uniquely trained and equipped to perform tactical (Special Weapons and Tactics) and technical rescue duty for other department elements. Members of ESU are cross-trained in multiple disciplines for police, first aid, and rescue work. In other words, they are elite cops, and the entrance to ESU's Truck 1 quarters was directly adjacent to the entrance to the 13th Precinct.

During a week of 4 x 12 tours I was assigned to teach during the last period of the evening. When I finished my class at midnight, the recruits were dismissed to go home. I was teaching in a fifth-floor classroom whose windows looked out on 21st Street. I have no idea what the subject was during that class, but I have a vivid memory of what happened during the class. About thirty minutes into the lecture I happened to glance toward the classroom door and noticed a uniformed cop standing outside the room, motioning for me to come out of the room. I initially thought it was someone from the police science department or recruit administration, but as I reached the classroom door I was surprised to see an ESU cop facing me. The cop had an extremely annoyed expression on his face as he said. "Here, I think someone in your class lost this." He handed me an apple core. I stared at the apple core with my mouth wide open. I was mortified.

The cop had been standing with another ESU cop outside their quarters on 21st Street when he was struck by the falling piece of apple. I felt uncomfortable asking, but the cop relieved my tension by explaining that he had already checked all the academy floors, and that this was the only room above Truck 1 that had any activity in it. I apologized profusely and then returned to my classroom. I could feel my hand shaking as I held up the apple remnants and asked, "Who did it?"

I imagine my wide eyes and shaking scared the class because there was complete silence. No one owned up to the act or implicated anyone else. I reasoned that it had to have been someone in the last row closest to the windows, but that mattered little to me. I ordered the entire company to return roll call after class. At the return roll call I ranted that because of the embarrassment they had caused me, return roll calls would continue until further notice. By the next day, however, I had cooled down and realized that I did not want to keep myself after work for fifteen additional minutes, so I canceled further return roll calls.

CHAPTER 12: MY RECRUITS

No English – No Problem

I had a very interesting experience with a recruit in my second cycle through recruit training. After completing the entire police science curriculum once, it was time to take a deep satisfying breath. The hard work was over. I had developed all my lesson plans and visual aids. Now, there would just be the fine tuning of several topics to make them work better in the classroom.

The second class did present some new frontiers. I was assigned two companies instead of one, and I was also the official company instructor, or OCI for one of the companies, meaning I was responsible for all administrative functions for the company.

During my first cycle I learned the names and faces of my recruits within two days. It was easy. I was only assigned one company and I had no OCI responsibilities to divert my attention. With my new OCI responsibilities as well as two companies to teach, I found that getting to know my recruits and recognize names and faces was taking significantly longer.

There are always recruits who will immediately stand out in the classroom for both positive and negative traits, but these easily identifiable recruits are the minority. Most recruits sit back in the classroom and do their work – quietly, without drawing attention to themselves. Such was the case with John. John was a 24-year old

Hispanic male who seemed very pleasant and cooperative, but he never said a word in class.

During the first few weeks of class there were several written homework assignments that had to be completed and handed in. These assignments were short essays that asked for the recruits impressions and experiences of some of the topics we were getting ready to cover. This was 1986, so there were no home computers or laptops to utilize. I did not even mandate a typewriter. I allowed the recruits to handwrite their assignments as long as the work was legible. During those first weeks John turned in several handwritten assignments that were correct in substance and impeccably written.

After a few weeks in the classroom I was able to get a read on who were the recruits who were always looking to participate in class and who would have to be dragged into the discussions. I didn't like to make recruits feel unnecessarily uncomfortable, but I wanted to get everyone involved in the class. As the weeks wore on I would make it my business to call on those recruits who never raised their hand in order to get them involved in the class. This technique worked well, and for some recruits, once I forced them to open up I could not get them to shut up.

John, however, was a problem. I had called on him a couple of times, and when he failed to respond I let him off the hook by calling on another recruit for the answer. On this particular day, however, I was not going to let John escape. We were discussing the dangers of reflexive response. There had been many instances where a police officer responded to a dangerous, stressful situation with his or her gun drawn. If one officer in the group fired a shot, there was a reflex that caused the others to immediately fire their weapons, not because of a perceived threat, but because of the sound of the shot. I was asking the class about how they felt about this phenomenon, and I went right to John for his opinion. John smiled meekly and halfheartedly shrugged his shoulders, but said nothing. I paced back and forth in the front of the room imploring John that he had to have some opinion on the subject. Again, I received only a weaker smile and shrug in response. I was quickly becoming annoyed. It was one thing to be shy, but his refusal to give his instructor a response was bordering on insubordination. One more time I asked for his opinion and one more time I received only an uncomfortable facial expression. That was it. I motioned for John to follow me out to the hall. Once in the privacy of the hall, I let John know how I felt about his silent act. I was ranting on and on about how his inability to respond in the classroom would be completely unacceptable in the street. I was becoming increasingly frustrated when I noticed the company sergeant had exited the classroom and was watching the action from a distance.

"Yes, what is it?" I snarled.

"Can I speak to you sir? It's important."

Michael was a twenty-eight-year-old navy veteran, and a very low key, but competent recruit. His maturity made him ideal for the role of company sergeant, and as the class progressed I appreciated his abilities and insights more and more.

Michael's body language was clear that he did not want to have our conversation with John, so I walked to him. "Well, what is it?"

Michael took a deep breath. "I was debating when I should tell you this, but I guess the time is now."

I waved my arms to the side. "Tell me what?"

"John doesn't speak a word of English."

"What?"

Michael nodded. "A couple of days ago one of the Spanish speaking officers in the class told me."

I was confused. "Then how could he……"

Michael knew my question and cut me off. "His wife did everything for him. I don't know how he was able to pass the civil service test – maybe he can read a little English – but from that point on, any documents he had to write during the background investigation and during your class were written by his wife."

I turned and looked toward John. He was about twenty feet away, still sporting his sheepish smile. I shook my head and told Michael to go back inside the classroom before motioning for John to follow me into the room.

As soon as the police science class was over, I went directly to the lieutenant in Recruit Administration in room 610 and informed him of the revelation regarding John. The lieutenant chuckled and said that John had come to him before muster that morning and attempted to resign. If he had come to resign I did not understand why he had just been present in my class. The lieutenant explained that he was instructed by the Chief of Personnel's office at One Police Plaza not to accept John's resignation. Apparently, the Department did not want to lose a minority recruit from its ranks, even if the recruit could not speak English.

I had no idea how the Department planned to deal with a non-English speaking recruit because the situation quickly became moot. Regardless of the Department's refusal to accept his resignation, John had other plans. When he departed the academy at the end of his tour that day, he never came back. He never answered any phone calls and I heard the Personnel Division actually sent someone to his house, but that he refused to see them. Finally, the Department had to comply with their own policy and consider that John was officially resigned after being absent without leave (AWOL) for twenty days.

Over Before it Started

During my two years as a recruit instructor I trained many young cops who I knew would turn out to be fine police officers and effective police leaders. There were two recruits, however, who never got the chance to have successful police careers. These two had their dreams terminated while they were in the academy. I don't feel sorry for anyone who commits a crime, but sometimes you have to look at the totality of the circumstances to see if there is something more to the story. In the cases of these two recruits, I couldn't help but feel sorry for them.

Larry was from Massapequa, or East Cupcake as we usually referred to the recruits hailing from Long Island. He tended to be reserved in the classroom, but he was always pleasant and cooperative and seemed to get along well with his classmates. It was a little past the halfway point in the academy class when Larry was absent on a Monday morning. It wasn't unheard of for recruits to be out sick, but the academy administration made such a big deal about being present for every academy class, approximately 95% of the recruits completed the academy without missing a day.

During my police science class, I noted Larry's absence on the attendance roster, but thought no more about it. Later in the tour I was sitting at my desk in the police science office when Sgt. Sean asked me to come into the supervisor's office.

Detective Caldwell was looking for my impression of recruit Larry. It seemed that Larry had been arrested by the Nassau County Police Department the night before. An arrest for any offense is career suicide for an academy recruit, but I was shocked to learn that Larry had been arrested for public lewd. I wasn't sure how receptive he would be, but I asked Detective Caldwell if he could share the details of the arrest. Caldwell shrugged and said "Sure."

It seemed that at about 8PM the previous night a 42-year old female was driving alone in her Toyota 4Runner in her home town of Garden City. When she stopped for a red light, the woman said that she glanced out her driver's window to the sedan that was waiting for the light in the adjacent lane. The woman said she was horrified when she noticed that the driver of the adjacent vehicle was smiling up at her while he stroked his exposed penis. When the light turned green the sedan accelerated away at a high rate of speed, and the woman attempted to pursue. At some point the woman said she was able to get the license plate number of the vehicle and she followed it for over two miles until it pulled into the parking lot of the Roosevelt Field Mall. The woman called 911 from a pay phone and confronted the driver of the vehicle in the mall parking lot. When the police arrived, they found the woman browbeating a very confused looking Larry. The patrol cop transported Larry back to the precinct and Detective Caldwell conducted an interview.

Detective Caldwell sat back in his chair and stretched. "I feel really bad for the kid," Caldwell said. "My gut tells me he's being sincere when he says he doesn't know what the lady is talking about."

"If you believe Larry," I replied, "then why did you collar him?"

Caldwell shrugged and extended his arms to the side. "What could I do? I had a complainant, and not just any complainant. This woman is an Assistant District Attorney in the Nassau County DA's Office."

I shook my head. "Isn't it possible that right after the vehicle sped away from the light she momentarily lost track of it and picked up on a different vehicle."

"Of course, it is," Caldwell replied. "But I know this lady and she is adamant that she identified the correct party." Caldwell shook his head. "This is terrible if the kid didn't do it. He'll get nothing for a bullshit public lewd charge, but I'm pretty sure he's done with the NYPD."

Caldwell glanced at the sergeant, prompting Sean to say, "Damn right he's finished."

As bad as I felt after my conversation with Detective Caldwell, I felt much worse two days later. I was walking down 20th Street returning to the academy with a Tasti-D-Lite frozen dessert in hand, when I suddenly stopped in my tracks. Larry was approaching in the opposite direction. We exchanged uncomfortable greetings before I asked the most ludicrous question imaginable - how's it going?

Larry shrugged, sighed deeply and told me his side of the story. He said that on Sunday night he was driving to the Roosevelt Field Mall to visit a friend who worked in a sporting goods store. Larry said that he was driving on Stewart Avenue as he approached the mall entrance and that everything was normal until he parked and exited his car. He said that as soon as he began walking from his car this woman came running up to him screaming about what a pervert he was and how he was not going to get away with it. Larry said that a crowd was quickly gathering as he told the lady that he had no idea what he was talking about. He said that the woman yelled to the crowd that Larry had just been "waving his dick at her." Larry said he was glad to see a Nassau County Police vehicle arrive because the crowd was becoming hostile toward him. He said he was stunned when the cop snapped handcuffs on him and placed him in the back of his vehicle.

Larry looked at me through moist eyes. "I swear to you I didn't do this. I never saw that lady before and I have no idea what she was talking about."

"Fight it," I proclaimed.

Larry shook his head and told me what I already knew. "Even if I beat it in court, a probationary police officer can be terminated for no reason. Let's face it - I'm finished with the NYPD."

I shook hands with Larry and tried to be encouraging, but deep down I knew he was right. I was one hundred percent convinced Larry did not expose himself to that woman that night, and that misidentification, however certain she was, cost Larry a career. Larry's story still bothers me today.

In the next class I had another recruit who was removed before completing the academy. I had less sympathy for this recruit than I did for Larry, but nonetheless, I still felt bad for Jim.

Recruit Jim was a 22-year old from the Bayside section of Queens. He was short and stocky, and during the two months he was in my class, he was articulate and cooperative. One day while I was seated at my desk, Sgt. Sean approached me accompanied by two middle aged men in suits. Sean told me to accompany him and the two men to the library. I was understandably nervous because I thought the presence of the two men could have something to do with me. My anxiety increased once we were seated around a table in the library when Sean introduced the men as a lieutenant and sergeant from the Internal Affairs Bureau. I breathed a huge sigh of relief when the lieutenant explained they were present to interview recruit Jim. I was scheduled to go into the classroom in thirty minutes and they wanted me to direct Jim to the library once class began. That's all the information I needed, but surprisingly, they volunteered the reason they were here to see Jim.

It seemed that their IAB group was working a case involving a police officer who allegedly had an ownership interest in a Queens auto body shop that had ties to the Gambino organized crime family. In performing their background investigation on the body shop the investigators learned that several years earlier the owner of the body shop was a female named Linda Paladino. Linda was the daughter of Sam Paladino, a known Gambino associate. The NYPD had several allegations that the shop was being used as a chop shop - a location where stolen vehicles are brought to literally be chopped up so that the individual parts can be sold. None of the chop shop cases ever stuck, however.

The shop and personnel from the shop were also associated with many staged accident claims. In performing their due diligence, the IAB investigators ran every name they uncovered in the investigation in the NYPD data base to see if any of the names belonged to a member of the service. Lo and behold, recruit Jim's name popped. It seemed that Jim was a claimant in three cases of accidents that had been flagged by the insurance companies as suspected of being staged. On three occasions, cars owned by Jim were involved in accidents with cars owned by Linda Palladino on the street directly in front of the body shop. How's that for a coincidence. The final straw for Jim was what followed next. The IAB investigators obtained the insurance investigation files on these accidents involving Jim, and in each of the files there was a signed statement from Jim describing the details of each accident. In each of his statements, Jim stated that he did not know the owner of the other vehicle, Linda Paladino. Three accidents with vehicles owned by the same owner at the same location - very strange. The final nail in the coffin, however, was the next revelation from the IAB sergeant. Linda Paladino, the owner of the body shop and the vehicles Jim had collided with on three separate occasions had also been Jim's fiancé. During the time of the accidents Jim and Linda were engaged, yet Jim declared in his written statements that he did not know Linda.

When I directed Jim out of the classroom that day, I knew I would never see him again. This was different than the situation with Larry. Jim made his bed, and now he was going to have to sleep in it - but I still couldn't help feeling bad for him. After all, as I illustrated in an earlier chapter, history, as well as the Police Academy is filled with examples of men committing incredibly stupid acts for the sake of a woman.

CHAPTER 13: ROLE PLAYS

The recruit punched out a red barreled revolver and shouted "Police! Don't move!" The male who was the focus of the red barrel was frantic, waving his arms and screaming that he had just been robbed and that the cop was letting the perpetrator get away. The recruit kept his weapon trained on the male and ordered him to lie face down on the ground, with his arms extended to his sides. The male protested vigorously, but eventually complied with the order. From the right side of the stage, the shout of "Cut!" ends the scenario.

Was the male the victim or the perpetrator? Should the recruit have ordered the male to the ground? These and many other questions would be subsequently answered in the critique of the role play.

In role plays, which took place throughout training, sometimes in class and sometimes before the entire assembled squad, the student officers faced the kinds of distressed people and enigmatic or volatile situations they would likely encounter on the street. The scenarios addressed the urgency, rawness, and spontaneity of the street. Role plays provided a superb opportunity for recruits to develop their skills as cops interacting with the public, closely approximating what they would soon be called upon to deal with every day.

Police work has been described as 90% boredom with the remaining 10% being sudden bursts of stress and fear. The role plays were meant to prepare recruits to handle the 10%. But they were simulations, and no matter how realistic they were scripted, they could never stimulate the actual physiological responses that would occur during one of these real situations.

As soon as a person feels fear, the amygdala (a small almond-shaped organ in the center of the brain) sends signals to the autonomic nervous system (ANS), which then has a wide range of effects. The ANS kicks in, and suddenly, the heart rate increases, the blood pressure goes up, the breathing gets quicker, and stress hormones such as adrenaline and cortisol are released. The blood flows away from the heart and out towards the extremities, preparing the arms and legs for action. The ability to think and reason decreases as time goes on, so thinking about the next best move in a crisis can be a hard thing to do.

A role play regarding the response to a man with a gun can be scripted with an amazing amount of detail, but at the end of the day, the recruit in the role play ultimately is aware that it is a simulation and does not experience the aforementioned physiological responses. So, the question became – can anything be done during academy training to stimulate the actual physiological responses to fear. The simple answer – you have to scare the recruits. But how do you do it in a safe, controlled environment. Answer – the stress exercise.

During the first week of training, all the recruits were given a drug test. Once the results of these tests were in, and it was confirmed that there were no failures, the stress exercise could begin. A squad sergeant from the three academic disciplines – police science, social science, and law, was required to enter a classroom in the middle of an instruction period. In his hand, the sergeant carried a folder that had boldly written on it "DRUG TEST FAILURES." The sergeant would stand in the front of the room making it very easy for the class to see the writing on the folder. He would then somberly read out five pre-selected names from the recruit company and instruct them to quickly gather all their belongings and come with him out of the room. After the sergeant and his group departed, the fear in the room was palpable. The most intense fear was reserved for the five who had been removed from the class and told they had failed the drug test, and that their careers were over before they began.

Sergeant Sean conducted the stress exercise with my company, boldly barging into my classroom while prominently displaying his folder. Sean dramatically called the names from the folder to the front of the room and departed with his devastated crew. I was left with a classroom now in a state of shock. After a few minutes I revealed the nature of the exercise to the class, and told them to think about how they were feeling, with their hearts beating faster and the anxiety they felt. I anticipated the return of the failing five, but when the class ended, the five recruits had not returned.

I returned to the police science office to find out what had happened. I found Sean sitting in his office working furiously on paperwork.

I stuck my head in and asked, "Everything go alright with the exercise?" The look on Sean's face indicated a complete lack of recognition. "The stress exercise," I clarified.

"Oh shit!" Sean blurted as he pushed past me and out of the police science office.

It seemed that while Sean was in the hall stimulating stress from the five recruits, a recruit from a different company ran up to him and reported that a different recruit had fallen in the cafeteria and was bleeding heavily from the head. Sean ran to the location of the injured recruit while leaving the five standing in the hall with all their gear, believing they had been terminated. Sean became completely immersed in the injured recruit and the ensuing paperwork. Until I stuck my head in his office, he had completely forgotten about the five recruits he had left hanging in the hall.

Now Sean was experiencing the physiological response to fear. The five recruits were gone. And why not. A sergeant had just informed them they had failed a drug test and were fired. When the sergeant ran off, what were they supposed to do? They went home. The lieutenant chairman of the police science department was also undergoing physiological changes. His responses, however, were not limited to fear. The lieutenant had an awful lot of anger coming through - anger directed at Sergeant Sean. The lieutenant did not care who heard him lashing out at Sean. "How could you be so stupid!" – "What if they jump in front of a train?" The lieutenant's physiology did not return to normal until all five recruits had been contacted. What about Sean? That was the great thing about him. The next day he was back to normal – ego fully intact. In his mind, he had administered the ultimate stress exercise.

A well designed role play could have an extremely positive effect in bringing the procedures and tactics of police science to life in a real-world scenario. On the other hand, a poorly designed role play could have disastrous results. There were interdisciplinary role plays that were scheduled into the curriculum and included aspects of all the academic subjects. Instructors were also encouraged to integrate role plays into lessons wherever they would be appropriate.

I integrated several role plays into my police science classes and they usually had a very positive effect on the training. One role play, however, didn't go quite as planned.

Even though most of police science consisted of policies and procedures, there were tactical subjects mixed throughout the curriculum. One such tactic was the use of cover and concealment. The difference between cover and concealment is a simple one. If it doesn't stop a bullet, then it is considered to be concealment because that is all it is really doing – concealing your location. Cover is something that will not only conceal your location but stop a bullet as well. Obviously, in facing a threat the recruits were trained to seek a position with cover. If no cover was available, however, we taught that concealment was better than nothing at all. Psychologically, shooters are looking for a clear line of sight from their gun to their target, and there is a tendency to avoid shooting into an object, even an object that a bullet will easily pass through. There are numerous documented cases where police officers have been saved by holding up an item like a wooden clipboard in front of the shooter, causing the shooter to try to shoot around the clipboard.

Like most of the instructors, I quickly developed my own role play kit. I bought couple of toy revolvers and a rubber knife and painted them all red. For the lesson involving cover and concealment I set up a very simple role play. I briefed two recruits as my actors. One actor was a hostage and the other was the shooter holding the hostage at gun point. The shooter had a red gun and I gave a red gun to the recruit playing the role of the patrol officer. The role play was designed to test more than cover and concealment. We had just covered the topic of responding to people in crisis, so I wanted to simulate an incident with a gunman and a hostage, both of whom are in crisis and danger. The responding officer will have to protect his life and the lives of the other participants while communicating with the perpetrator and victim, requesting assistance on his radio, maintaining tactical cover and/or concealment, and using deadly physical force if necessary. It was a lot for the responding recruit to comprehend, but I wanted to emphasize that this was the type of scenario they could face on the street that would require a wide range of split-second decision-making.

I took the patrol officer recruit into the hallway and briefed him. He would enter the classroom as if he was on solo foot patrol and had just turned the corner of a street. He would be required to deal with whatever situation he discovered when he entered the classroom. The actors playing the gunman and hostage were placed on the side of the room near the windows, as far from the classroom door as possible. I gave the shooter a red gun and told him to stand behind the hostage with the gun pointed at the hostage's head. I provided the hostage very simple directions just cry and keep pleading for the officer to help him. My direction to the gunman were a bit more complicated, but still very simple. I instructed the gunman to keep the officer engaged in conversation, but not to comply with any of his instructions. Let me repeat this because it is important to the story – I told the gunman actor NOT to comply with any of the responding officer's instructions.

With the gunman and hostage in place at the far side of the front of the classroom, I stuck my head into the hall and said "Action." When the responding officer entered the room, and observed the gunman holding a hostage, he immediately did the right thing by seeking cover. He drew his red revolver and stood behind a coat rack that I had labelled "Tree." In a loud command voice, the officer shouted, "Drop the gun!"

So far, so good. As soon as my responding officer observed the situation, he sought cover, drew his weapon and engaged the gunman with a clear command. I was curious to see when the responding officer would go to his radio to request assistance. I'm still curious because the role play never got that far. Remember I told you that I specifically told the gunman not to comply with and directions of the responding officer. Well, what do you think the gunman did as soon as he was commanded to drop the gun? That's right, he dropped the gun. Correction – he didn't just drop the gun. He placed it on the floor and slid it to the responding officer. If that wasn't bad enough, what do you think the responding officer did when the gun reached his position. Did he leave it on the floor and keep his own gun trained on the perpetrator? No! Did he pick up the gun and secure it on his person? No! As soon as the gun slid to the responding officer, in one fluid motion this recruit calmly slid the gun back to the perpetrator. I was dumbfounded. It looked like a shuffle board game at the front of the classroom. All I could do was wave my arms and yell "Cut!" I approached the responding officer and shouted, "What the hell did you do?" He just shrugged and said, "I didn't think you wanted the role play to end so quick, so I gave him his gun back." Thankfully, it was time for the class to end.

My best role-play story was not mine, but was related to me and other instructors as a lesson on how not to conduct a role-play.

When one thinks of the NYPD, they immediately think of police officers – and rightfully so. The New York City Police

Department, however, employees thousands of workers who are not sworn officers. The NYPD employs doctors, lawyers, architects, intelligence analysts, criminalists, 911 dispatchers, medical assistants, computer specialists, school safety officers, and police administrative aides, to name a few. There are even hostlers working for the NYPD. What's a hostler, you might ask? Hostlers care for horses and maintain stables and equipment in the NYPD mounted units.

Besides training police recruits, every now and then instructors would be given additional responsibilities with some of these work groups that required some elements of Police Academy training. police administrative aides, or PAAs, for example, were civilian personnel hired by the NYPD to perform clerical and administrative duties in the precincts and specialized commands. PAAs had to receive training in all the department forms and paperwork utilized by police officers. Another NYPD job title that many people were not aware of was police attendant. These civilian employees were hired to search, guard and look after prisoners and detainees at the precinct and central booking holding cells.

Every precinct has holding cells and each borough had a central booking facility to process arrests in that borough. Prisoners were transported from the precincts to central booking where they were processed for arraignment in court. If the prisoners were not going to make it to arraignment while court was still open they would be sent back to the precincts to be lodged overnight. The attendants were responsible for the safety and security of the detainees while they were in these NYPD holding facilities. The attendants received a two- week course at the Police Academy regarding the history and structure of the department as well as instruction in the department paperwork they would be utilizing. Because of their job description, and their contact with prisoners, a heavy emphasis during the training course was placed on searching.

When I was given the assignment to instruct a two- week class of ten newly hired police attendants, PO George, the police science curriculum coordinator and one of the more veteran instructors at the academy, took me aside to give me a word of advice. George tried to be as diplomatic and politically correct as possible in relating that many of the attendants came to the job with experience on the opposite side of the cell bars. I don't know if you get the picture, but I knew exactly what George meant. He further told me that it would seem like common sense for an instructor to run role plays with the new attendants that involved searching, because searching prisoners would be one of their more important roles. As relevant as these type role plays would be, George cautioned against the idea. He told the story of an instructor who had been assigned to an attendant class a couple of years earlier. George said that when the lesson involving searching techniques came up he broke the class of ten into two groups. Five of the trainees would play the role of prisoners while the other five would be attendants. He said that the instructor loaded the prisoners with all types of simulated weapons, secreting, guns, knives, and drugs under all areas of their clothing. The five other trainees were then instructed to conduct thorough searches of their prisoners. The lesson to be learned with this role play was to show how easy it was to miss weapons and contraband during a search. George said that the instructor walked back and forth behind the trainees as various weapons were removed from the prisoners. When all the attendants indicated they had completed their searches, the instructor called off the exercise. Now, George continued, was when the instructor would show the trainees how many guns and knives they missed. Several weapons were in fact missed, and after the point had been made and the role play completed, George said the instructor gathered up his stock of simulated weapons and sent the students on a break. George smiled and said there was one big problem the instructor did not anticipate. Among all his toy guns and knives, he found a real, loaded 38 caliber, 2-inch revolver. One of his students had been carrying an illegal gun that had been uncovered during the search. George said it was easy for the instructor to determine the owner of the illegal gun because when his class returned from their break, one student was missing. George put his hand on my shoulder and said that the moral to the story was not to do the search role play with this group of employees.

    I took John's advice and skipped the search role play. I did have a very positive experience with the attendants during their two weeks of training. At the end of the police recruit classes, it was traditional for the companies to show their appreciation to their instructors by giving them an authorized gift – usually a plaque. I still have some very beautiful plaques given to me by my recruit companies. When I completed the two weeks with the attendants I had no expectation of a gift, but at the end of the final day of class, a spokesman for the group of ten came to the front of the room with a bag, and said that they had a small gift to show their appreciation for my efforts. I opened the bag and pulled out a baseball cap from the White Castle hamburger restaurant chain. For those unfamiliar with White Castle, it is the burger chain famous for the small square hamburgers affectionately referred to as "Belly Bombers."

What did a White Castle cap have to do with police academy training? I still don't know. I graciously accepted the gift, said thank you and wished them all well in their careers.

CHAPTER 14: GRADUATION

Graduation is a huge day in the life of a police recruit. It is the culmination of months of hard work and the final transition from the world of academia and theory into the real world of the street. Graduation is also a big day for the academy instructors as they get to pridefully sit with their graduating company.

I had already experienced graduation from an academy as a trainee twice, with both experiences having their own unique aspects. My first experience was graduation from the Border Patrol Academy at the Federal Law Enforcement Training Center in Georgia.

The intense Border Patrol training was over and graduation day had finally arrived. I proudly strode towards the FLETC auditorium in full dress uniform, a huge feeling of pride overcoming me. Like most of the FLETC complex, the auditorium was shiny and new. The stage, seating, and wood trim all had that very new, unused look. Throughout the sixteen weeks we had lost two classmates, so on this mild February Southern Georgia morning, thirty members sat proudly in the first two rows of the auditorium, ready to receive their US Border Patrol shields.

I sat in silent anticipation as the dignitaries on the dais began to populate the stage. There were high ranking personnel from both the Border Patrol and FLETC, as well as all the FLETC and Border Patrol instructional staff. Speeches commenced and awards were given to the class members with the highest academic, physical, and firearms scores. Next, the members of the graduating class were called to the stage one at a time to receive their shields and two graduation certificates. One certificate was for completion of the Border Patrol Academy and the other was for completion of FLETC's Police Training Division.

I was back in my seat with my precious loot safely in hand. I took a deep breath while the closing speech of a high-ranking Border Patrol official provided background noise. I glanced around to try and savor the moment. As good as I felt I could not help but notice the very odd nature of this graduation ceremony. Surrounding the crowded dais and graduating agents was row after row of empty seats. The entire auditorium was empty. No one came to watch the graduation ceremony. In retrospect, I don't know why I found this peculiar. After all, I never expected my family to make the trip from New York City to Georgia for a one-hour ceremony, and I guess the other families from all over the country felt the same way. Still, it was the first and only time in my life that I was part of a graduation or promotion ceremony that no one attended.

My graduation from the Transit Police Academy was more traditional. The ceremony for the 420 new police officers was held in the auditorium at Brooklyn College, with the venue packed to the rafters with friends and family members. What made this graduation ceremony unique was the subsequent schedule. The Transit Police Department had no real field training program for new academy graduates at the time, but they masked this deficiency by assigning the graduates to rotating squads in the districts for two weeks. During this time the new officers would be assigned to work with a veteran cop who had no training, and usually no desire to work with a new cop. For the Transit Police Department, this qualified as field training.

Transit Police rotating squads worked on a four days on – two days off schedule. For each four-day work period, the shifts rotated from 8AM x 4PM to 12AM x 8AM, to 4PM x 12AM. District and squad assignments were made randomly, and it was simply the luck of the draw as to when a new graduate's first tour of duty would be after graduation. For some lucky officers, their assigned squads were finishing up a set of midnight tours on our gradation day. This meant they transitioned right into two days off and did not have to report for duty until 4PM on the third day. This left plenty of time to celebrate graduation and revel in the accomplishments of the prior six months. I was not quite so lucky. I was assigned to District 20 in Queens, and my squad was on its second regular day off and would begin a set of midnight tours the next day. In realty, when I got home at about 2PM after the graduation and a celebratory lunch with my family, I had to report for duty at District 20 at 11:25PM. Welcome to police work.

My graduation ceremony at Brooklyn College was impressive, with speeches by the Chief of the Transit Police Department and the Chairman of the Metropolitan Transportation

Authority, but I had always been envious of my NYPD brethren because the NYPD Police Academy graduation ceremonies were usually held at New York City's famous Madison Square Garden. I have to admit that after my first class as an instructor, I was as excited as my recruits at the prospect of sitting on the garden floor and looking up at thousands in the crowd, sharing the view captured nightly by members of the Knicks and Rangers as they ran and skated up and down the court and rink.

About a week before graduation my dreams of basking in glory on the floor of Madison Square Garden were dashed. Much to my chagrin, only OCI's would sit with their companies. Since I was not an Official Company Instructor for this class, I was assigned other duties for the ceremony.

I was assigned to manage the VIP seating section. After six months of teaching new recruits how to be police officers, I was going to be an usher at Madison Square Garden. It was approximately an hour before the graduation ceremony was to begin, and I had assumed my post at the VIP section. The gates of the Garden were just about to open, so at this point all the seats, including my VIP section, were empty. I took a moment to reflect on how great the seats in this section would be for a hockey game. I ceased my evaluation of the seats when I heard noise from behind me, indicating that guests were about to enter my VIP section. I turned and walked up a couple of steps, but then stopped abruptly. Coming down the steps towards me was Deputy Chief R.

Deputy Chief R. was the executive officer of Patrol Borough Bronx. He was a huge man of both height and girth, and his protruding forehead gave him a very Cro-Magnon look. Six months earlier I had witnessed Chief R. basically assault an academy sergeant at One Police Plaza.

On Zero Day, the recruits traveled to police headquarters at One Police Plaza in Lower Manhattan. The purpose of the expedition was a visit to the Equipment Section on the first floor for equipment issuance. I was not an OCI for this class, but I was directed to accompany Sgt. A with his company to see how the process worked.

Everything appeared to be progressing well – at least to me it did. The recruits lined up quietly, money orders in their hands, waiting to enter the Equipment Section to be issued: two pairs of dark blue trousers with black stripes down the side, blue tie, gold tie clasp, reflective belt, nameplate holder, two nightstick straps, whistle, whistle holder, baton, baton holder, rubber billy, two belts, handcuffs, handcuff case, gun cleaning kit and cloth, pen and pencil holder, memo-book cover, first aid book, two speedloader cases, and an academy bag to carry it all in.

Maybe he hadn't liked the way the recruits were standing in line, or maybe he just wanted to make an impression on them, but whatever the case, Chief R. began by giving Sgt. A a good dressing down right in front of his recruits. Sgt. A. was trapped with his back against a wall, while the Chief, a good foot taller than the sergeant, hovered menacingly over him, wagging his right index finger mere inches from the sergeant's nose. Sgt. A later told me that all he said was "Please don't put your finger in my face, Chief." Chief R. immediately complied and removed his finger from the sergeant's face. Instead, he grabbed Sgt. A with both hands by his collar, and literally lifted him off the ground while slamming him several times against the wall. The Chief released his hold and the sergeant almost fell to one knee. The finger retuned to Sgt. A's face for one last time as Chief R. warned "Let that be a lesson to you." before departing the building for his return to the Bronx.

Sgt. A. was almost hysterical, ranting about assault, having the Chief arrested and initiating a lawsuit, none of which ever happened.

As could be expected, Chief R. had made a huge impression on me, so it was with a sense of terror that I watched the Chief pay me no mind as he removed a roll of electrical tape from his pocket and proceeded to tape off six seats, obviously being reserved for guests of his. After completing his taping job, he ascended the steps and was gone. For about one second I actually considered removing the tape, but common sense quickly got the better of me, along with visions of six months earlier. If the Chief had no problem throttling and slamming a sergeant against a wall, there was no telling what he would do to a mere police officer.

It was at this time that Sgt. Sean arrived in the VIP section to check in on me. This was the same Sgt. Sean from the police science department who made critical remarks on my classroom evaluation, even though he was asleep. Sean was a nice enough guy, but he liked to portray himself as a no-nonsense tough guy, which he wasn't.

"How's it going?" Sean asked as he surveyed the conditions in the empty VIP section.

"Not bad." I responded, completely ignoring the presence of the taped off seats.

Sean, however, was not ignoring the tape. "What the hell is that?" Sean stated in an irritated tone as he pointed towards the unauthorized reserved seats.

"A chief taped the seats off." I responded.

"Did he have authorization?" continued Sean.

"I have no idea" was my prompt response.

Sgt. Sean shook his head in obvious disappointment in my inability to control my assigned area. "This is bullshit. When he comes back, tell him he can't reserve seats in the VIP section."

Sean began to walk away, but before he could I committed the first and only act of blatant insubordination throughout my entire career. "Nope" was the single word that stopped Sgt. Sean in his tracks.

"What did you say?" the sergeant snarled.

I completely understood the insubordinate nature of my remark, so I quickly explained, "With all due respect sarge, it was Chief R. who taped off the seats."

Sean shot back in his most macho tone "I don't care what chief it is. If you don't have the balls to confront him, I will."

At this point I would have enjoyed watching Sgt. Sean get throttled by that big goon, but I actually liked Sean, so I had to say something "Don't you remember what happened to Sgt. A?"

The blank look on Sean's face made it clear that he required further information. "Remember on Zero Day when Sgt. A. was roughed up. Well, it was Chief R. who slammed him against the wall by his collar."

Sean brought his right hand up to his chin, striking a thoughtful pose. He was obviously trying to think of a face saving strategy. "You know, half these VIP seats are never used so there's no reason to hassle a chief over a non-issue, right?"

I nodded my head in agreement "You are absolutely right, sir. Thanks for your help."

CHAPTER 15: THE RUBBER BAND DOES ITS JOB

I have mentioned many benefits to working at the Police Academy, but one I did not reference was the exceptional environment it provided to study for promotional exams. Even though I was teaching from the NYPD patrol guide, I still had tons of time to study the Transit patrol guide during my non-classroom hours. My studies paid off, and early in 1988 I was promoted to sergeant. I was thrilled to be promoted, but there was a bittersweet aspect to be leaving the Police Academy.

I had been a patrol sergeant in District 4 for about a year, and I was beginning to look for that rubber band that was supposed to bring me back to the Police Academy. When I finally got the opportunity, I hooked myself up and readied myself for the trip in the elastic band that would sling me directly to the Police Academy. I must have hooked up to the wrong rubber band, however, because this one shot me directly to 300 Gold Street. The Transit Police Academy operated its in-service and specialized training operations out of 300 Gold Street, while its recruit training personnel were detailed to the NYPD Police Academy.

Captain O, the commanding officer of the Transit Police Academy explained to me in a thick Irish brogue that he desperately needed an administrative sergeant, and if I labored in that capacity for a while, he would send me to 20th Street at his earliest opportunity.

I never took to the role of administrative sergeant, and it didn't help matters that Captain O. was a pain in the ass, or should I say *arse*, to work for. The most glowing compliment I received from him was when he described me as being like one of those children's punching bags. He stated "Lad, every time I knock you down, you keep bouncing back up for more." I guess that was a compliment.

The normal administrative responsibilities involved overseeing the civilian clerical staff, maintaining the record of the building inventory, maintaining academy training records, processing and securing department identification cards, and anything else that the captain wanted me to do. It was during this time that William Bratton arrived as the Chief of the Transit Police Department and a transformation of the Transit Police Department began.

Conferences and meetings with different police departments and organizations became frequent events, with the large open sixth floor at 300 Gold Street becoming the usual conference center. It was pretty much universally agreed that morale was up with the members of the Transit Police Department. Everyone's morale except mine, that is. All those meetings and conferences had to be catered, and Captain O. decided that it would be my job to perform the catering function. Almost overnight, approximately 75% of my job became catering meetings, conferences, and ceremonies. I was given a staff of one to handle these events that were becoming more and more frequent.

Police Officer Bill was a cop on restricted duty due to a leg injury. Bill wanted to be called "Crash" due to his penchant for getting into car accidents, which was the cause of his leg injury. Crash was a small, wiry 32-year old with a bushy mustache who walked with a noticeable limp. He had been born in Georgia, and even though he moved to New York City while still a child, you could still detect a very slight trace of a southern drawl in his voice. The arrival of Crash just added to my depression. The prospect of being the Department's maître d was humiliating enough on its own. Now, I would have to do the job with a hillbilly gimp sidekick. My initial assessment of Crash could not have been more off base. He turned out to be one of those rare people who actually seem to understand life, with the ability to differentiate between what is truly important and what is nonsense. In fact, I credit Crash with not letting my Police Academy rubber band snap, which would have resulted in me being instantly catapulted back to patrol.

My first event was an easy one, and I completely screwed it up. The Chief of Patrol made a reservation to use one of Gold Street's conference rooms for a staff meeting. Besides the Chief of Patrol, there would be approximately fifteen chiefs and inspectors attending. A meeting like this required a set-up of just coffee and donuts. Just before the meeting I ran up to a supermarket on Myrtle Avenue to buy the donuts, and while walking back I remembered that we were low on cups, so I detoured to a wholesaler who was located a block away from Gold Street. Just before the meeting started, Crash set up the coffee pot and arranged the donuts decoratively on several trays. At the last minute, I ran in with the cups. The meeting began and catering catastrophe struck. Now, it is very important to remember here that I have never drank coffee throughout my entire life. To me, paper cups were paper cups. I never considered for a moment whether I was buying hot cups or cold cups. Crash suddenly appeared at the administrative office door and told me that we had to go to the meeting immediately. When I entered the conference room I observed in horror that every attendee, including the Chief of Patrol, had a large puddle of coffee on the table in front of them. I had purchased cold cups which the coffee just burned right through. Crash worked his way around the table with a towel while I ran across the street to Franks Sandwich Shop and bought fifteen cups of coffee. Once I was back with the coffee it appeared that the situation was under control and I could take a breath. About an hour later the meeting was breaking up so Crash and I readied ourselves for the post meeting cleanup. Just down the hall from the conference room I could see Captain O. engaged in a conversation with the Chief of Patrol. Based on the body language, I did not perceive the conversation to be cordial. A minute later, Captain O. was striding down the hall towards me. Again, based on the body language I could tell that he was not seeking me out to offer congratulations. Most of the donuts I had put out for the meeting where of the white powder sugar variety. At the conclusion of the conference, most of the chiefs and inspectors had blotches of white powder staining their dark blue uniform blouses. The captain had just been dressed down by the Chief of Patrol, and you know what they say about shit rolling downhill. One statement stood out from the captain's tirade that lasted for several minutes. At one point he blasted me with "You can't be selectively stupid, lad!" An hour later I was sitting with crash in the administrative office, mired in the depths of my depression. I was a police sergeant who had just been crucified by my commanding officer over coffee and donuts. I had had enough, and I was going to tell the captain such. Before I could complete my self-destruction, Crash gave a short speech that changed my perspective and kept my academy rubber band from snapping.

"Hey, this job sucks and is humiliating. We both know that. But you still want to go to the 20th Street academy, and the only way you're going to get there is if the captain sends you there. In the meantime, whether we like it or not, we are going to be the Department caterers, so why not be the best caterers that we can be."

That corny speech got to me because Crash was absolutely right. I did want to teach at 20th Street, but I was on the verge of blowing that opportunity over coffee and donuts. From that moment on, if I had to be the department caterer. I would be the best caterer.

The change in our attitude and operation was immediate and noticeable. It even reached the point where the impossible occurred when I was able to convince Capt. O. that he was wrong regarding the food for a catering job.

The Chief of the Department was hosting a large contingent of police officials from Moscow and a part of the week-long festivities was going to be a breakfast reception on the 6th floor at Gold Street. Captain O. wanted Crash and me to travel to the Brighton Beach section of Brooklyn, a predominantly Russian neighborhood, and pick up a wide assortment of Russian pastries and breakfast foods. I told the captain that this would be a huge mistake.

"If we went to Moscow" I rationalized "would you be happy if they served McDonald's"

The captain gave me that pensive stare that always kept me guessing as to what he was thinking. Finally, he responded "You may be right, lad".

We ended up laying out a hot buffet of eggs, bacon, sausage, and potatoes. What kept me from enjoying a brief moment of triumph, however, was one final humiliation endured by Crash. It was not enough to lay out the donuts and pasties next to the buffet. Capt. O, broke out a hors d'oeuvre tray that I did not know we possessed, and he insisted that Crash circulate through the room in dress uniform and white gloves, offering donuts and pastries to the guests. I was mortified, but again, Crash kept it all in perspective. "Who knows", he mused "If I'm able to eventually get off the job on a disability pension, I'm getting on the job training for a new career."

As the calendar passed into December, I finally had the one conversation with the captain that I had been looking forward to for over a year. He informed me that he was sending me to the NYPD Police Academy for the next recruit class in January. Salvation was in sight, but I had one more catering job, and it was going to be the mother of all my catering jobs.

The Transit Police Department, as well as the NYPD, traditionally had promotions just before the holidays. The Chief of the Department announced there would be promotions to various ranks during the week before Christmas, and that the promotion ceremony would be in the courthouse inside Brooklyn Borough Hall. The Chief got the idea to use Borough Hall because a restoration of the building had just been completed, making it look like it did when it opened in 1848 as the then-city of Brooklyn's City Hall. The building was one of New York's finest Greek Revival structures—and Brooklyn's oldest public building. Outside, a triangular pediment of white Tuckahoe marble steps sat under six grand columns and a handsome Ionic portico. Inside, a two-story rotunda enveloped visitors with more marble columns, gray-and-white floor tiling, and pink marble walls. There were also plenty of remnants of the building's previous functions as a court and jail: defunct holding cells, caucus rooms, and most impressively, a magnificent courtroom that would be used for the promotion ceremony. A week before the ceremony I was feeling pretty good because I believed Crash and I had covered all bases for the event. We were ready, and I was ready for the rubber band to pull me to 20th Street a week later.

I had no idea why Captain O. wanted to see me in his office, but I knew it must have something to do with the ceremony. "The Chief was doing a walkthrough of the courtroom at Borough Hall, and he took note of the grand piano in the room."

Unfortunately, I had an idea where this conversation was leading as Captain O. continued. "The Chief thought it would really be a nice touch to have holiday music played on the piano before and after the ceremony."

"That would be nice," I commented, "but where are we going to get a piano player?"

The captain displayed his small, somewhat evil smile "I think you can figure that out lad. Sgt. K. tells me that your wife is an accomplished pianist."

I was verbally agreeing that my wife was a wonderful pianist, but my mind was focused on kicking Sgt. K in his butt for volunteering that information to the captain. Of course, I endured the final humiliation of supplying my wife to play the piano at the promotion ceremony. Actually, she was thrilled to play, and everyone, including the Chief of the Department was thrilled with how well she performed. I, on the other hand, had to suffer the indignity of the jokes pointing out that I was such a kiss ass and lackey, that I would even supply my wife to the Department.

Just before the pre-ceremony performance concluded, Captain O. pulled me aside and placed something in my hand. "Get some flowers for you wife lad" he said as he thrust fifty dollars into my palm.

As the captain walked away, and evil thought entered my mind. I was finally receiving some monetary recompense for my humiliation. I had absolutely no intention of getting my wife flowers. This $50 was going to be a humble reward for all the crap I had endured.

The ceremony proceeded as planned and at its conclusion, my wife was on again for her post-ceremony concert. Everything was right with the world. The world quickly turned upside down however, when Capt. O told me to have the flowers ready in five minutes because the Chief of the Department wanted to personally present them to my wife. What could I do? I certainly couldn't tell him that I pocketed the money. One more time it was Crash to the rescue. He took the money and hobbled –ran out to the street. Just as my wife was finishing her last song, a heavily breathing Crash appeared holding a bouquet of flowers. I am no flower aficionado, but this was the most pathetic looking bunch of flowers I had ever seen. My initial reaction was "Are you serious?", but Crash cut me off "Hey, just be thankful that the religious cult was outside."

I had to agree, but I also asked for the change "What change?" Crashed snapped back

"You paid $50 for those" I said pointing to the bouquet in which half the flowers appeared to be already dead.

"Hey, I'll take them back if you want," Crash stated sarcastically.

My wife received a standing ovation while holding the bouquet. Across the room, I received a bouquet of daggers straight from the eyes of the sneering Captain O.

Two weeks later, the rubber band did its job and pulled me back to the 20th Street academy. In my mind, I was home. All was right with the world. It was during this time as a sergeant at the NYPD Police Academy that I began working closely with Sgt. Bill.

I met Bill while we were both recruits in the Transit Police Academy at 155th Street. We were in the same recruit company for a little more than half of the six-month academy session. Our academy class was hired in October, and as I previously described, the conditions in the former grammar school were less than ideal for police recruits. My class of 420 recruits packed the building completely, but the Department wanted to hire approximately two hundred more cops, and for reasons known only to the Department, they could not wait until we graduated in March to hire the next class. They hired the two hundred new recruits in January and stuffed them into our already crowded building. How was the department able to jam "ten pounds of potatoes into a five pound bag," you might ask? Simple, they just consolidated recruit companies.

I was originally in company 7 with approximately twenty other recruits. Bill was assigned to company 8. When the consolidation occurred, company's 7 and 8 merged to form a new company. This was a very simple process on paper, but the reality was that classrooms that had been accommodating twenty recruits now had to house forty. Every square foot in the building was used for classroom space – even the locker rooms.

Bill and I were in the same consolidated company after January. I didn't really know him then, but I got to know him very well once we were both assigned as academy instructors. Bill was one of the most unique characters I ever met and he was also a great friend. As a police officer, Bill was assigned to the NYPD Academy six month before me, and he was also a police science instructor. My first real experience with Bill occurred during the recruit evaluation meeting.

A few weeks before the final trimester examination, the Commanding Officer of the Recruit School would meet with all the instructors to identify recruits who may have problems with graduation due to poor academic grades, physical training grades, or disciplinary issues. This was really a forum for the official company instructors to comment on the status of their recruits. I was not an

OCI during my first class as an instructor, but all instructors were required to sit in on the meeting.

The meeting was conducted in a classroom, and the format was very simple. The Commanding Officer would start with company 1, and the OCI would comment on any recruits he or she felt might have problems attaining an overall passing academic grade. The physical training instructors provided similar feedback for their grades, and the academy Integrity and Discipline sergeants commented on the disciplinary records.

It didn't take long for me to realize the unique nature of Bill's character. The OCI from company 1 began his commentary on a recruit who had had problems on the first two trimester exams. The recruit's name was Jackie Robinson and the OCI expressed confidence that the recruit had been performing better in class which he felt would manifest itself in a good mark on the third trimester exam. Before the Commanding Officer could move on to the next company, Bill's distinctive voice sung out from the back of the room. "Looks like Jackie Robinson will slide home safely."

Bill then threw his head back and laughed manically at his own joke. Everyone else in the room, including the Commanding Officer was silent, cautiously staring at Bill to ascertain if he was in the middle of some type of seizure. Eventually, decorum returned and the meeting continued.

Normalcy prevailed until the Integrity and Discipline sergeant brought up a recruit who was being processed for termination as the result of being arrested off duty during the raid of an illegal massage parlor. Anytime a recruit was going to be terminated, it was not a time for jokes, but this was Bill in the audience. Without missing a beat, he called out, "Looks like this story won't have a happy ending."

Again, Bill lapsed into red-faced hilarity while the rest of the room looked on in horror. As I would soon learn, this was simply a case of Bill being Bill.

The recruits loved Bill. He had several routines that he used in the classroom, one worse than the next. One of Bill's favorite routines was to walk into the classroom carrying a newspaper – not just any newspaper, but the New York Post. At some point during the class he would toss the newspaper onto the floor and stand next to it. He would then point at the class and declare, "You never want to be caught in my position."

There was the pregnant pause while the class waited for it, with Bill finally giving it to them. "You never want to be caught off post."

Just to make sure everyone in the class understood his pun, Bill would then step onto the newspaper and state, "You always want to be on your post."

One of Bill's more tasteless acts was extremely visual, but I will do my best to paint the verbal picture. At least with the off-post routine there was some type of connection to police work. This classic had no segue at all. Out of the blue, Bill would suddenly declare "This is my impression of Tom Carvel taking a dump."

For those who don't know, Tom Carvel was the founder of Carvel, the famous ice cream franchise. Bill would stand in the front of the room, get into a semi-crouch and gyrate slowly at the hips. I realize this is a tough one to visualize, but think of the last time you went into an ice cream store and ordered a soft ice cream cone. The worker will position the cone under the ice cream machine and rotate the cone so that the ice cream falls into the cone in a nice swirling design. Bill was simulating the same swirling design of the substance flowing from his butt if he were actually performing the bodily function. Like I said – tasteless – but funny.

The bottom line was that Bill conducted a vaudevillian, high-energy class – maybe a little too high energy, but the recruits loved him.

I made sergeant about a year before Bill, so by the time Bill's rubber band pulled him back, I was already at the NYPD Academy. Sergeant's at the academy had several roles. They functioned as supervisors for the academic and physical training departments, but they could also be assigned as instructors. Sergeants were also assigned to Recruit Administration to supervise the daily administrative issues concerning the recruits and the instructors.

For years, Recruit Administration had been on the sixth floor of the academy in Room 610. 610 was where student officers had to report if they were late, didn't follow instructions for sick leave, or for any other problems that may arise. Reporting to 610 was like going the school principle, except here, with an irritated police lieutenant or sergeant doing the reprimanding and a career at stake, it was more disconcerting. Indeed, the recruits came to loathe reporting to Room 610.

I had been assigned to Recruit Administration, which had been relocated to the fifth floor in Room 523. The NYPD, Transit Police and Housing Police had desks in this huge office which still functioned as the hub of recruit training activities. For the recruits, just as it had been with Room 610, a successful six-months at the academy meant staying as far away from 523 as possible.

It might not seem like such a big deal to change locations and room numbers, but 610 had come to mean more than a room number. No one ever said, "Report to Recruit Administration." It was always "Report to 610." 610 had become part of the lexicon of the Police Academy, so when Recruit Administration relocated to 523, the majority of the staff still referred to the location as 610. As a matter of fact, some industrious staff member covered the 523 above the office door with a homemade 610 sign. All was right with the world again.

I would much rather have been a sergeant assigned to teach recruits in the classroom, but instead I was dealing with the daily recruit problems in 610....I mean 523. Fate placed me back in the classroom and back in close contact with newly assigned academy Sgt. Bill.

You might recall I previously mentioned an incident where several female recruits and male instructors got into hot water – literally – when one of the recruit's NYPD ID cards was found in the bathtub of a sleazy Manhattan hotel. When the hotel clerk found the ID card, he promptly notified the NYPD, and at the end of the weekend the terrified recruit was spilling her guts to one of the academy Integrity and Discipline sergeants.

The instructors were immediately launched back to patrol commands for violation of the Police Academy fraternization policy. These transfers created an immediate problem for the Transit Police contingent at the Police Academy. The police science instructor taking a bath had been a transit cop, and now the Transit Police had to cover the void left by the instructor's departure. This bathtub incident occurred with four months still remaining in the academy class, so a new instructor would have to be inserted into the company. Since I had been a police science instructor I was immediately assigned to the instructorless company while Sgt. Bill was brought in to take my spot in 610....I mean 523.

It was during this time period that I got to know Bill well. One of my vivid memories of Sgt. Bill involved the command log. The sergeant assigned to the recruit operations desk was responsible to maintain the command log during the tour. The log was a chronological account of events. Some were routine, with entries being made every tour regarding how many instructors and recruits were present. Entries also had to be made for any incidents that occurred. Recording these incidents in the log was where Sgt. Bill was at his best.

Bill was a news buff. I take that back – he was well beyond a buff. Bill was obsessed with the news. He could tell you the broadcasters on every network news show, as well as the time slots for news reporters on the radio. He also knew all the television and radio news jargon used by reporters in their telecasts. I loved to read his command log entries for an incident because as I read the log, I would think I was watching the six o'clock news.

For example, if a recruit twisted his ankle while running in the gym, Sgt. Bill's log entry would begin, "Things took a bad turn for recruit officer Smith today when he twisted his ankle while running in the gym."

In a twist that was even more bizarre, Bill would routinely filter in lines from his favorite TV show when he was a kid – Superman. In using a Superman line, he described an incident when a recruit fainted during muster. "During the muster today, recruit officer Smith fainted while in company formation and was removed to Cabrini Hospital for treatment. At the time of the incident it was hotter than the hot seat at Sing Sing."

Sgt. Bill's command log entries made it painfully obvious that no one actually read the log because no one ever said anything to him about his entries. Bill had a lot of fun with another academy record he was sure no one read. Recruits had to use the stairs to access the six floors of the recruit section of the academy. They were not permitted to use the elevators unless they had a doctor's note documenting a need to use the elevators. The actual process required the recruit to appear with the doctor's note at Recruit Administration where a sergeant would review the documentation and issue an elevator pass for an appropriate period of time. The elevator pass was a card that the recruit was required to keep on his or her person while they were authorized to use the elevator. The card contained basic information including the recruit's name and the dates the elevator pass was active. There was also a line on the bottom of the card for an authorized signature. This was the line where a sergeant from Recruit Administration had to sign for the elevator pass to be authorized. Sgt. Bill was convinced that no one ever looked at the authorized signatures on the elevator passes, so he had a lot of fun with those passes as only Sgt. Bill could have.

Bill started off by signing elevator passes based on the recruit's condition. Dr. Scholl's is probably the most well-known name in foot care products. Whenever a recruit would have a medical condition regarding the foot, Sgt. Bill would sign "Dr. Scholl" on the elevator pass. When Bill became bored with Dr. Scholl and other medical related names, he began using the infamous Nazi Doctor Mengele as the authorized signature. I remember counselling Bill that it might not be such a good idea to be signing the name of a Nazi on an academy record, so he again changed strategy. He began using the very juvenile approach to humor with signatures of Ben Dover, Mike Hunt, and Hugh G. Rection. If you're not getting the humor in the last name – keep saying it – you'll get it.

Sgt. Bill traveled through life with the simple philosophy of never taking anything too seriously. Couple that attitude with a propensity to break out in uproarious laughter at the drop of dime, and you got some very entertaining optics whenever Sgt. Bill was around. Take, for instance, Sgt. Bill's relationship with Sgt. Ed, one of the academy Integrity and Discipline sergeants.

The Integrity & Discipline Unit, or IDU was the academy's police. Working under the aegis of the Commanding Officer of the Police Academy, the unit handled all investigations that were reported to it, and maintained records of all recruits and academy instructors, who were also not immune to disciplinary action from IDU. The lieutenant and five sergeants assigned to IDU worked in plainclothes, and could pop up anywhere around the building or in the geographic area of the Police Academy, to enforce the rules of the NYPD and the academy.

IDU had their own office adjacent to room 523, but they maintained a desk in Recruit Administration so that they could deal with daily recruit issues outside of their office. Prior to the beginning of a tour of duty, Sgt. Ed would sit at the Integrity &

Discipline desk and torture recruits who were either summoned to see him, or who had requested to see him. The Integrity & Disciple desk was only about ten to fifteen feet from the Transit Recruit Operations desk, so Sgt. Bill was able to hear every encounter between a recruit and Sgt. Ed. The recruits were terrified of Sgt. Ed, and he played his role very well. I suppose being an officious prick came very naturally to him. Sgt. Bill reaped great joy in listening to Sgt. Ed's rants and usually bursting out in inappropriate laughter. One incident that Bill found particularly funny was when a recruit was standing at attention in front of Sgt. Ed's desk, and Sgt. Ed began the interaction by declaring, "How dare you interrupt me before I've had my muffin."

Sgt. Ed was having a heck of a time maintaining his tough guy image with the recruits with Bill cackling with laughter every time Ed was disciplining a recruit. They were both sergeants, so there wasn't much Ed could do about it. I remember once Ed approached me and inquired about Bill by asking, "What exactly is wrong with that guy? Does he have some mental condition?" I just shook my head and Bill went right on being Bill.

Bill's favorite Sgt. Ed story, and the tale that had the longest lasting effects, involved one of Ed's internal academy investigations. It was during one of the rare occasions when Ed was holding court in the instructor lounge, detailing the results of one of his investigations. It seemed there had been a couple reported thefts from the male gym locker room.

When the recruits reported for their physical training classes, they would first travel to the locker room to change into their physical training uniform before reporting to the gym. All recruits were required to have a combination lock to secure the locker while they were inside the gym. On two occasions recruits reported they had money removed from inside their wallets while they were in the gym. In both instances the recruits found their combination locks open and they both said it was possible they did not properly secure the locks.

Ed said that he set up a locker with the clothing and property that would typically be inside while a recruit was attending a physical training class, including a wallet with cash. He said that he placed a combination lock on the locker door but did not secure the lock.

I have no idea how Sgt. Ed maintained surveillance of the locker since just about everyone knew you could not put a camera in an area like a locker room where people would have a reasonable expectation of privacy. Whatever investigative technique he used, Ed failed to catch the thief. As a matter of fact, he dejectedly stated that the only activity he observed was someone masturbating in front of a locker. Everyone in the audience laughed, but Sgt. Bill was turning beet red from his laughter. To break Ed's balls a bit, one of the other sergeants asked if he intended to discipline the recruit he observed. Ed sat up straight and threw his head back. "Recruit?" he scoffed. "It was a staff member."

Sgt. Bill literally fell to the floor with Ed's revelation. Ed would never reveal the identity of the person, but from that moment, continuing to today, I just have to mention, "It was a staff member" to Bill and hilarity ensues.

CHAPTER 16: THE WRONG REVIEW MATERIAL

Academy life went on as normal for the remainder of that class. I continued instructing my two companies in police science and Sgt. Bill continued laughing in Recruit Administration.

There was a female recruit in one of my companies who I knew was going to have a difficult time passing academically. She had failed the first two trimester exams and I didn't see much hope for her in the third and final trimester exam, even though she appeared to be working as hard as she could. The recruit actually passed the third trimester exam, but because the final grade was an average of the three trimesters, her first two failing exams scores pulled her overall grade below the minimum grade, despite the fact she had passed the final exam.

The recruit was obviously depressed with the outcome, but I explained to her that hope was not lost. The academy had a hold over program. Instead of graduating and reporting the patrol commands throughout the city, these recruits who had failed to achieve an overall passing grade were placed in the holdover program. The holdovers received an additional month of classes to review the entire curriculum before taking administered another exam. The results of the holdover exam were then averaged in with the scores of the three trimester exams, and if the overall average was above the passing minimum, the recruit was graduated. If the average including the holdover exam did not reach the required score, the recruit was processed for termination.

A sergeant from police science, law and social science was responsible for providing the question bank to the testing unit from which the holdover exam would be developed. Although they would not know what the specific questions on the exam would be, these sergeants knew what topic areas would be on the exam. This information was critical because these sergeants were responsible for providing the review curriculum to be presented to the holdovers during the final class before the exam.

In the police science department, Sgt. Sean was responsible to provide the question bank and the review curriculum. You remember Sean, don't you? He was the sergeant who would fall asleep in my classes when evaluating me, but then make critical remarks on the evaluation sheet despite the fact he was unconscious during most of the class.

I was extremely disappointed when the holdover exam grades were posted and I observed that my recruit had failed. It was doubly disappointing to see that she had actually passed the sections of the exam on law and social science, but an extremely low grade on the police science section had sealed her fate. I really had no great desire to see this recruit, but several hours after the grades were posted she sought me out in Recruit Administration.

The recruit was a very young, petite, black female, and it was obvious from the moist condition of her eyes that she had been crying. There was no sense piling on, so I approached her as if she had lost a family member – I told her how sorry I was. The water works around her eyes began operating again, but I was not focusing on her tears. I was much more intent on grasping what she was saying. The recruit was adamant about how hard she had studied for the test, and that her efforts had been reflected by the grades she received in law and social science. She continued to say that she had studied just as hard for police science. I cut her off and stated the obvious. If she had studied so hard for police science, how could she possibly have gotten such a lousy grade. The recruit wiped her eyes and said that nothing that was presented in the police science review was on the exam. I stared at her silently for a moment before asking her to repeat what she had said. She repeated that none of the police science topics she had studied from the review class were on the exam.

Most administrative processes in the NYPD were slow, and the process to terminate a member of the service was no exception. Once a recruit had failed the academy it took several weeks for the recruit to actually be terminated. During those weeks the recruit was directed to report to the Police Academy in recruit uniform, and was assigned clerical tasks to perform.

I told the recruit to hang loose, and that I would look into the holdover exam and see what I could find out. My next stop was with Sgt. Joe in the academy testing unit. He gladly let me see the police science question bank Sean had provided, and the actual police science portion of the holdover exam. A review of the question bank and exam revealed that all the police science questions on the exam came from the provided question bank. I knew I could not remove any materials from the testing unit, so I asked Joe if I could return in a few minutes to take a second look at the same documents. He shrugged and said "Sure," so five minutes later I was back in the testing unit holding a copy of the police science review curriculum Sean had provided to the holdover recruits.

My mouth opened wider and wider as I compared the review to the exam. Oh my God, the recruit was correct. None of the questions on the exam were on topics provided in the review.

I found Sgt. Sean snoozing in the police science office. I woke him and explained the situation. Sean did not seem overly concerned. He shrugged and commented that recruits are responsible for all the material and not just the material in the review curriculum. I was becoming frustrated with Sean's attitude. I explained that it just wasn't right to tell a recruit to concentrate on studying topics A,B and C only to give the recruit topics X,Y, and Z on the examination.

Eventually, Sean recognized the problem. I think I finally got to him when I said that a recruit was being denied a police career because he had given her the wrong review curriculum. To his credit, Sean had no problem admitting his mistake to his superiors. Within a week, the recruit was given another review session and another holdover exam. This time she easily passed. Tears were flowing again, but this time they were tears of joy.

Several weeks later I received a letter of thanks from the NYPD Guardian Association. The Guardians were the fraternal organization for black members of the service. The president of the guardians expressed his thanks for my diligence in seeing that a potential career ending wrong was righted. I was grateful for the thanks, but the recruit's race or fraternal affiliation had nothing to do with my actions. The recruit could have been purple and I would have done the same thing. Wrong is wrong in any color.

CHAPTER 17: BREAKING AWAY

My tenure as a sergeant assigned as a recruit instructor ended after my extended substitution period. For the next class I was back at the transit recruit operations desk in 610....I mean 523.

Big things were beginning to happen in the Transit Police Department during 1992. In 1990 Bill Bratton arrived from Boston and made a huge impact in establishing an identity for the Department, other than the historical subservient role of little brother to the NYPD. No longer did the Transit Police respond and copy NYPD initiatives – the Transit Police Department became innovators. Transit police officers transitioned from revolvers to 9mm semi-automatic pistols well before the NYPD. Even subtle uniform changes, like the authorization of the commando sweater, had an immensely positive impact on morale.

The commando sweater, in particular, caused some tense moments at the Police Academy. There may have been various words to describe the problem the NYPD had with the Transit Police commando sweater, but the word I felt was most appropriate was jealousy. The commando sweaters were sharp-looking, and since they had not been an authorized NYPD uniform article, only the Transit Police instructors could wear the sweaters while mustering the recruits. This jealousy resulted in the NYPD academy recruit operations management issuing an edict that Transit Police instructors were forbidden from wearing the commando sweaters. The transit cops and sergeants quickly called their unions (PBA and

SBA) and within a day we were still mustering the recruits in our commando sweaters.

For years there had been talk of a merger of the NYPD, Transit and Housing Police Departments in New York City. Bratton had been against a merger and had taken numerous steps, such as the 9mm pistols and commando sweaters, to help the Department establish its own unique identity. In 1992 Bratton returned to Boston and the reigns of the Transit Police Department were handed over to Mike O'Conner, a career transit cop. O'Conner continued to fight the ever-increasing gravitational pull towards a merger by pulling the transit police out of any joint initiatives with the NYPD.

Since 1983 recruits hired for NYPD, Transit and Housing all trained at the New York City Police Academy. Recruits were mixed together in the recruit companies and instructors like myself were mixed throughout the recruit training school. Chief O'Conner took the bold step of announcing that in 1993 the Transit Police Department would operate its own Police Academy and would no longer train alongside the NYPD.

The new Transit Police Academy was actually the old Transit Police Academy. 300 Gold Street was a 6-story building located in downtown Brooklyn, near the intersection of Flatbush Avenue and Tillary Street. The building was erected sometime around 1900, and it had functioned as a shoe factory until the Transit Police took it over during the 1950's. Several of the Department's administrative units had offices in the building, and several classrooms had been built to house the Transit Police Academy. Even during the years of recruit training at the NYPD Police Academy, the Transit Police Department conducted in-service, promotional, and specialized training in the building. Some administrative offices were relocated out of the building to create more classroom space, but the new Transit Police Academy would be in the same old ex-shoe factory.

The facility was only half the job of opening a new academy. Now we had to have a recruit curriculum to teach. I was designated to be the chairman of the behavioral science department. Behavioral science was the exact same subject matter as social science, but to maintain our unique identity, the subject was given a different name. I was give this role because I was the only sergeant on staff with any experience with the curriculum. During my last class as a police officer instructor, before I was promoted to sergeant, I had switched from police science to social science, so I had been through the social science curriculum once. This extensive experience labelled me as the most qualified sergeant on staff for the role of behavioral science chairman.

Over the next six months I single handedly developed the New York City Transit Police Academy behavioral science recruit curriculum. Wait a second! Before you reach the conclusion that I was some type of dynamic curriculum guru, let me explain what the process of curriculum development consisted of. Ninety nine percent of my curriculum development involved paging through the NYPD social science student guide and changing every reference from New York City Police Department to New York City Transit Police Department. Additionally, I had to change the header from Student Guide – Social Science – New York City Police Academy to Student Guide – Behavioral Science – New York City Transit Police Academy. The final act of plagiarism was the most complex. I had to transitize every chapter. For example, in a social science chapter detailing how to handle a domestic dispute in a home with sensitivity and compassion, I would change the setting to a husband and wife fighting on a subway platform.

The only real innovation I inserted into the curriculum was ultimately stolen from me. As I went through what was essentially a massive cut and paste job, I was smart enough to realize I was going to have to come up with at least one topic that was mine, and that I hadn't just copied from the NYPD social science curriculum.

I had spent two years working on the Mexican border in the United States Border Patrol, and during my training and working environment I had become conversational in the Spanish language. I recognized the value of New York City cops being able to communicate in Spanish, but I also understood that the Police Academy was different from the Border Patrol Academy, where several hours each day was spent in intensive study of Spanish. A central tenet of the Border Patrol training, however, was memorization. Being immersed every day in a work environment where Spanish was the primary language spoken was the fastest way to develop fluency, but this competence did not develop overnight.

There were certain key Spanish words and phrases that were used daily that had to be memorized during training, and one of the requirements to successfully complete probation was passing an oral test involving these phrases.

I used this same memorization principle in developing a Crisis Spanish lesson plan. The lesson had two parts. The first part required recruits to memorize Spanish words and phrases that would be important during a stressful patrol situation. It did not matter if they understood the conjugation of the verbs and the tense of the sentence – they just had to be able to pronounce the words correctly. The phrases required for memorization were presented in the student guide in three columns. The first column was the English phrase. The second column was the same phrase in Spanish, and most importantly, the third column displayed the phonetic pronunciation of the phrase.

In total, there were fifteen phrases the recruits had to memorize. During the final testing process, they had to pass a one on one oral exam in which they could correctly speak all the phrases.

Part two of the lesson involved the use of Spanish words and phrases on memo book insert cards. The theory was that not every interaction with a Spanish speaking person was going to be a life-threatening emergency where split second action was required. Still, the non-Spanish speaking officer could still have a positive impact on the situation by being able to perform basic communication. In these non-stressful situations, the officer would be able to refer to a series of memo book insert cards to find the proper Spanish words and phrases for a particular situation.

Frankly, I probably put more work into developing this Spanish curriculum than I did in cutting and pasting the rest of the lessons. By the time the police merger occurred in 1995 I was a lieutenant and no longer involved with recruit training. In fact, the merge snapped my rubber band permanently, and I was never assigned to any branch of the police academy for the remainder of my career. When the merge took place, most of the transit recruit instructors were sent along with the recruits to the NYPD Police Academy to complete their training. About a year after the merge I ran into one of the instructors who had been in my behavioral science department, and who had returned to the social science department in the NYPD academy. We made some small talk and of course I asked how things were going with the recruit training. He shrugged and complained a little about the social science department. I guess a cop wouldn't be a cop unless he had something to complain about. Suddenly, he snapped his fingered and his eyes widened as if a light bulb had just appeared over his head.

"I know what I wanted to tell you," he began. "They stole your Spanish lesson."

"What?"

"That's right," he nodded." "They did a cut and paste job. All they did was change New York City Transit Police Department to New York City Police Department."

For an instant I was incensed. How dare those bastards plagiarize my hard work. Very quickly, however, reality set in. What a hypocrite I was to be upset. I had done the exact same thing with the NYPD social science curriculum, and now I was on the receiving end of a copy and paste job. I guess I deserved it.

Before the Transit Police Department went out of business, I was still the behavioral science chairman at the academy for the inaugural recruit class in January of 1993. This was an exciting time. All the hard work in putting together a full-service recruit training school finally came together when 154 recruits were hired, including 19 recruits from the Metro North Police Department and 9 from the Long Island Railroad Police Department.

The hiring day was an operational challenge in itself. This was the day the personnel about to be hired were handed off from the Applicant Investigation Unit to the Police Academy. I had been through several hiring days while assigned to the NYPD Police Academy, each with its own unique challenges. For two of the hirings the Transit Police instructors were pulled back to the Transit Police facility at 300 Gold Street, and all the Transit Police recruits were hired separately. The following day, the recruits and the instructors reported to the NYPD Police Academy to be blended in with the NYPD recruits and instructional staff.

There were other hirings where NYPD, Transit, and Housing recruits were hired together. One of these hirings stands out in my mind for a completely different reason. I believe it was around 1992 when I was back at the NYPD academy as a sergeant. I may be getting some of these details wrong, but I believe it was the hiring of the July class, and as a matter of fact, I think the class was scheduled to begin academy training on July 1st. Very shortly before this date, it was communicated to the NYPD that for some fiscal and/or budgetary reasons, these new recruits had to be hired before July 1st. I'm not certain how many recruits were in this class, but it was well over a thousand. These soon to be police officers were directed to report to a public high school in Brooklyn at 11PM on June 30th. The recruits were sworn in before midnight to satisfy the mandate to hire before the end of the month, and the remainder of the night was used to process paperwork and give introductory speeches, just like any other hiring day. It was weird to be releasing over a thousand new recruits in business attire for their meal hour at 3AM. The Commanding Officer of the Recruit Training School breathed a huge sigh of relief when he was informed that all recruits were accounted for at 4AM after the meal period was over.

Let me return to the hiring day for the first class at the new Transit Police Academy in 1993. The hiring of these 154 recruits took place at PS 248 in Brooklyn.

By virtue of its name, PS 248 had been a New York City public school and still looked like just about every other public school built in New York City in the early and mid- 20th century. The building, which was located at Avenue X in the Bensonhurst section of Brooklyn, had been used as a Transit Authority training facility for at least a decade.

Everyone had a role on this day. The commanding officer of recruit training division gave a welcoming speech followed by an introduction to the subjects they would be studying. I gave a brief speech regarding the behavioral science curriculum followed by Sgt. Bill, who gave the same speech for the police science department. After similar speeches regarding law and physical training the recruits were ushered from station to station for various paperwork, forms and ID card photos.

Lt. Vinny was the executive officer of the Recruit Training Division, and he was operationally in charge of the entire hiring process. I had come on the job with Vinny in 1981, and besides working for him at the academy I also considered him a friend. Vinny was one of the most competent people I encountered during my career and he was also one of the funniest. Vinny was also friendly with Sgt. Bill, and he was well aware of Bill's somewhat off-center personality, so even under the most serious of circumstances, such as a police hiring, Vinny would not pass up the chance for a prank.

To the new recruits sitting stiffly in the auditorium, , Lt. Vinny seemed anything but a prankster. In rapid fire delivery, Vinny spelled out some of the more important rules of the academy -

lateness, sick procedure, inspection. When and how to stand at attention. How to address superior officers. Vinny told the student officers that the next six months would be demanding, and that their lifestyles would change dramatically. I noticed a few recruits grimace. It sounded like Vinny was trying to talk them out of becoming cops, and if that was the case, his speech worked. One tall recruit walked to the back of the auditorium, waved down an instructor and resigned.

The hiring day basically consisted of putting out one fire after another as the day wore on. From investigating recruits who had not appeared to be hired, to dealing with a malfunction of the ID card camera, to handling a line of duty injury for a recruit who tripped and fell in the stairway, there was one crisis after another to deal with.

We tried mightily to avoid a crisis involving parking in the area. The street parking near the site was tight, but being an old public school, the building had a huge schoolyard attached to it that would have been a perfect parking lot for the day. The Transit personnel running PS 248, however, did not want the recruits parking in the yard, so great lengths were taken to have the hiring notifications include the fact that they could not park on the site. Additionally, a police officer was posted at the entrance gate to the yard to prevent recruits from entering.

Sometime during the late morning a frantic looking Lt. Vinny approached Sgt. Bill and addressed him with a sense of great urgency. He told Bill that a recruit had somehow gotten into the yard and was blocking a transit truck from leaving the facility. Vinny handed Bill a piece of paper containing a license plate number and told Bill to go on the stage of the auditorium and announce the license number so that the recruit could move his or her car. As Bill hurried on stage, Vinny poked me in the side and said, "Watch this!"

Sergeant Bill trotted on stage and called a halt to whatever administrative task that was in progress. He grabbed the microphone and addressed the recruits seated in the auditorium.

"May I have your attention please. Would the owner of the following vehicle see me immediately – New York License number I-8-1-U-8-1-2."

There was silence in the auditorium, so Bill repeated the plate number. This time the silence was punctuated with a small sprinkling of laughter. Again, he read out the plate number. Finally, Bill realized what he was saying and nearly fell over laughing on stage. For those of you reading this who haven't gotten the joke yet, Vinny had successfully played one of the oldest and most juvenile pranks on Bill. He stood up on stage with the microphone, announcing to the recruits phonetically - *I ate one, you ate one too.*

Vinny made a science out of pranking Sgt. Bill, and Bill was always good natured about the jokes. Bill was very intelligent, but sometimes he would react before thinking. Such was the case with another of Vinny's pranks.

I did not live too far from Sgt. Bill, so when we began working out of Gold Street to prepare for the new academy, we worked the same hours and carpooled. We alternated who drove day by day and our unofficial ritual was to stop at a deli in Maspeth, Queens so that the passenger in the car could buy two beers for the remainder of the ride home. We always stopped at the same deli because it was just off the exit from the Long Island Expressway. I don't remember what the name of this deli was, but that was irrelevant because we called it by one name – the moustache. The owner of the deli was an older eastern European man with an extremely thick, bushy mustache – hence, the moniker.

After work on a day that I was driving I pulled to a stop at the curb in front of the moustache so Bill could buy our beverages. Just outside the entrance to the moustache was one of those old-school coin operated kiddie rides that were around since the 1930s. By the 1990s these rides weren't quite extinct, but you did not see many of them. When I was a kid these rides were everywhere. There were cars, trains, planes, and helicopters, just to name a few. They all operated the same way. When I was young, a dime was inserted and the ride shook back and forth or up and down. Inflation had raised the price to a quarter on the horse that sat in front of the moustache's deli. Bill emerged from the deli carrying a bag, but instead of returning to my car he hesitated next to the horse and waved to get my attention. When he was confident I was watching he put the bag on the ground, but removed one can of beer. He opened the can of beer before jumping onto the saddle of the horse.

He then inserted a quarter and the ride was on. As the horse moved up and down, horrified parents steered their kids away as Bill screamed "Yahoo" in between sips of beer. The optics of seeing this grown man riding the horse were hysterical.

The next day I told Lt. Vinny of the incident, and I could see almost immediately that his brain was working on a prank. By this time Vinny had enough experience with Bill to realize that his scheme didn't necessarily have to make sense for Bill to buy into it.

Approximately 15-minutes before the end of our tour, Vinny called Bill and me into his office. As we were getting seated I did not miss the wink and twinkle in Vinny's eyes directing me to go along with what he was going to do. With a concerned expression, Vinny shook his head and began. "I just got a call from the Queens North Borough office." Vinny didn't miss an effect. He looked momentarily at the paper he was holding in his hands. "I spoke to the Commanding Officer of Queens North Inspections – Captain Ferris." Another pregnant pause before Vinny continued. "Did you guys stop at a deli in Maspeth on your way home yesterday?"

"Yes," Bill and I answered in stereo.

Vinny continued. "Were you drinking and causing a disturbance at that deli?"

Vinny had thrown out the line and Bill bit right into the hook. "I wasn't causing any disturbance," Bill said with disgust. "I was just riding the horse."

"Riding the horse?" Vinny feigned confusion.

"Yeah, I was on the kiddie ride outside the deli."

"Were you drinking?" Vinny asked.

Bill shrugged. "Yeah, we always stop there for a beer on the way home – so what?"

Vinny threw the paper on his desk and threw his arms out to the side. "So – now I have to answer out to this captain why police academy instructors are making a scene on a public street, acting unprofessionally, while intoxicated."

Bill stood up like he had just sat on a tack. "Wait a minute, no one was intoxicated. As a matter a fact, I had just taken one sip from the beer."

"Just sit down and relax." Vinny motioned for Bill to sit. He then stared at the paper on his desk and buried his head in his hands. "I don't know what we're going to do here. I have to answer this out. This Captain Ferris isn't just any captain. He's a big wheel in Queens North."

Vinny stared directly at Bill. The twinkle had returned to his eyes, followed by a very slight grin. He shook his head as his smile became larger. "I guess I could keep this up forever if I wanted to. Let me ask you something, Bill. How would a captain know that you were a member of the service, no less a police academy instructor?"

Bill just shrugged and remained silent.

Vinny continued to painfully explain the prank. "And you never saw anything odd in the captain's name – Ferris – and he's a big wheel in Queens."

Bill slightly tilted his head, wrinkled his nose and squinted. He had no idea what Vinny was talking about.

Vinny shouted the punch line. "Ferris wheel, you idiot!"

Bill bent over in the chair, laughing maniacally – face red and feet stomping the floor. Yes sir, Sgt. Bill was one of a kind.

CHAPTER 18: THE LAST RUBBER BAND

I was promoted to lieutenant in February 1993, and as excited as I was, I have to admit to some regrets at leaving the academy again. The new police academy project had consumed everyone since the preceding summer, and now, a little more than a month after the inaugural recruit class began training, I was gone. I also was going to miss the working environment at the Gold Street academy. Working and carpooling with Sgt. Bill and being supervised by Lt. Vinny were some of the most enjoyable times I had during my career. On some days, my body would literally be aching from all the laughter.

My first assignment as a lieutenant was in the Bronx, in District 12. I spent a year on patrol before I was able to strap on my rubber band one more time. It had the elasticity for one more trip, but when it catapulted me out of the Bronx, it missed the NYPD academy in Manhattan and dropped me back at 300 Gold Street. This would be my last trip back to training. My rubber band had snapped.

I was back at Gold Street, but not back to the Recruit Training Division. I was the new commanding officer of the Educational Development Unit. EDU was responsible for developing and delivering all the in-service, promotional, and specialized training to members of the Transit Police Department.

As I settled into my new academy role, the drum beats were getting progressively louder regarding a merger of the police departments in New York City. At the same time, the command staff of the Transit Police Department was screaming louder and louder about how there would be no merger. During the final two years of the Transit Police Department's existence, the Chief of the Department and Transit Authority management took whatever steps they could in an attempt to create distance between the departments, even as the merger talks were bringing the departments closer and closer. In my humble opinion, the entire new police academy project was simply a tactic to pull the Transit Police away from the NYPD.

The merger denial in the Transit Police command staff continued to the bitter end. EDU facilitated the training of the last Transit Police promotions to sergeant and lieutenant, and I made it my business to sit in on the speech the Chief of the Department gave to the new promotees. The last Chief had been recently elevated to the job from Deputy Chief of the Department when the old Chief saw the inevitable merger writing on the wall and quit. During his speech to the sergeants and lieutenants, I realized that the new Chief still had his head buried in the sands of fantasy. Instead of telling the group to look forward to their futures as supervisors and managers in the NYPD, he told them stories about how the Transit Police was in the process of establishing a myriad of new specialized units, such as a crime scene unit.

I guess you can figure out by now that there never was a Transit Police Crime Scene Unit, or any other new specialized units. On April 2, 1995 the New York City Transit Police Department ceased to exist.

The period right after the merger took effect was unique, and in some aspects – bizarre. The first day the merge went into effect, I had a conversation with the civilian director of training of the Transit Police Department. Dr. O had come to the Transit Police a couple of years earlier after being a cop in Houston. He was a very nice man as well as being very competent. Dr. O was unsure of his fate in the NYPD. He showed me a letter he had received from the NYPD directing him to appear at the NYPD headquarters auditorium for orientation and assignment. This was obviously the form letter that was sent to the hundreds of Transit Police clerical employees, and now Dr. O feared that after being the director of training for an entire police department, he was going to end up typing complaint reports in an NYPD precinct. I laughed and told him not to worry and that it was obvious that the form letter didn't apply to him. I was right. Dr. O ended up being the Deputy Commissioner of Training for the NYPD. Unfortunately, the good doctor was way off the mark about my post-merger fate. During our conversation, besides contemplating the necessity to hone his typing skills, the doctor opined that I was in the best position to be retained by the NYPD Police Academy. He could not have been more wrong, and it took me all about an hour to realize my fate.

When the merger became a certainty, the Police Commissioner wasted no time in commencing all the necessary mechanizations. An NYPD department bulletin went out directing all unit commanding officers to meet with their Transit Police counterparts to discuss the seamless transition of the Transit operations into the NYPD. I had received a phone call the day before arranging a meeting at Gold Street with the inspector in charge of specialized training at the NYPD Police Academy. I attended this meeting alone while the inspector arrived with an entourage of nine lieutenants, sergeants, and police officers. It was less of a meeting and more of a discussion between the NYPD academy personnel regarding how they would utilize Gold Street. I was not necessary for this meeting, and obviously, I was not essential for NYPD Police Academy operations. The following day, all personnel who had been part of the Transit Police Training Bureau were transferred to the NYPD Police Academy at 20th Street, including all the recruit instructors and supervisors along with all the sergeants and police officers in my Educational Development Unit. Everyone from the Transit Police Academy was gone to the NYPD Police Academy – everyone except me, that is. My academy rubber band had snapped for good. I was heading for patrol and would not be returning to a training assignment for the rest of my career.

I used the word bizarre to describe the immediate post-merger environment. It certainly wasn't bizarre that I was not being retained by the Police Academy. What was very strange was how long it took to transfer me to a patrol command. When I signed into the command log at Gold Street the next morning, reality began to fully set in. Not only was my police department gone, the entire Transit Police Academy, except me, was gone to 20th Street. I was certain I could perceive a distinct echo from the emptiness as I strolled about the 5th floor academy facilities. Finally, I settled into my closet-like office and got down to the only business of the day; television watching.

My daily television marathons went on and on, and at one point I actually thought about staying home, but I rationalized that the day I decided to stay home would end up being the first time someone was looking for me. The situation progressed from the ridiculous to the sublime as four weeks passed, and still I sat at my desk working the remote. The only break from the monotony was provided on three occasions by NYPD academy personnel who came by to take measurements of some of the Gold Street offices. In one particularly ridiculous sequence academy staffers took measurements of my office while I sat at my desk watching TV. They worked their tape measure and made their notes without ever acknowledging my presence in the room. Finally, just as I prepared to sign out for completion of my fourth week in limbo, the call came in. I was transferred to Transit Bureau District 20 in Queens.

  In 1997 I was promoted to Captain, finishing my career in the Housing Bureau and the Property Clerk Division. When I reflect on my twenty years with the Transit Police / NYPD, I worked in a variety of assignments as I advanced from police officer to captain, including patrol, narcotics, internal affairs, the property clerk division and the auto pound. But I will always look back to one recurring assignment that characterized my career as well as some of my post retirement endeavors – the Police Academy.

EPILOGUE

About a year ago, business took me on a nostalgic journey. I am currently the Chief Security Officer for a New York State government agency operating within the confines of New York City. As such, I still maintain a strong partnership with the NYPD and interact with various members of the police department on a regular basis.

On this day, I was on my way to a training seminar being conducted by the NYPD. The subject of the seminar was irrelevant to me. It was the location of the training that brought back memories. I was driving to the new Police Academy in College Point, Queens. The three-spectral blue-and-gray structures hovering over the flat, industrial horizon near Flushing Bay had special meaning to me. First, it was the Police Academy, and I couldn't help but feel that the rubber band I was given so long ago was pulling me back one last time to see what it had evolved into. Second, the location had additional significance to me that had nothing to do with the Police Academy. The academy had been built on the site formerly occupied by the NYPD Auto Pound. I had spent the last year of my career on that site as the commanding officer.

An inspector was running the training seminar, and he began the session by providing the class a tour of the entire facility. The three structures that comprise the complex are an eight-story classroom and office building, with a seven-story atrium, an 800-seat cafeteria, an 800-seat auditorium and a two-story library; a physical and tactical training building with a 45,000-square-foot main gymnasium (a little more than an acre) and a 75-foot-long pool.

The academic and training buildings are linked by a glass-enclosed bridge over a drainage canal that was incorporated into the landscaping. A wide pedestrian link extends the length of the campus and gave me the feeling that I was walking through a large transportation hub like Grand Central Station.

The pride of the inspector's tour were the realistic simulated settings built for the recruits to train on. There was a full-size street scene complete with a bank, grocery store, and a bar with an awning that read "New York City Bistro." There were even lifelike trees in the scene made largely of recycled steel and composite material.

In another large room was a 2011 Chevrolet Impala police car and a Nissan Altima passenger car, mounted on dollies so an instructor could move them to demonstrate the proper position for stopping another vehicle.

In another area was a simulated Bronx subway station with a modified, but real, R-110B subway car stopped just beyond the turnstiles. Additionally, there were five different apartment layouts (bathroom signs caution, "Mock toilet, not for use"), as well as an L-shape apartment hallway and a mailbox vestibule; three precinct houses, each with holding cells and a muster room; and three different courtrooms — ornate Supreme Court, modest Criminal

Court and spartan Traffic Court — where recruit officers get a foretaste of testifying.

The facility was truly impressive, yet, I smiled upon noticing the touches that reminded me the project was still a product of New York City government. When I took this tour, the academy had been in operation for over a year, yet there were areas of unfinished landscaping all around the complex. The ugly, unfinished work made the Police Academy look like a beautiful woman wearing an evening gown that was stained and full of holes. Also, reflective of a New York City construction project was what wasn't at the site. I remember clearly when the project got its final green light to begin construction, the Police Commissioner gushed about how the new Police Academy would be the gold standard for police training in the 21st-century. Besides the actual academy structures, the site was also to include a firearms range and a driver training track so that recruits would no longer have to travel to the Bronx and Brooklyn to receive firearms and driver training. The Commissioner also talked about a five-star hotel that would be part of the academy complex allowing police dignitaries from around the world to take part in NYPD training and be lodged on site.

Well, recruits still travel to Rodman's Neck in the Bronx for firearms training and to Floyd Bennet Field in Brooklyn, for Driver Training. As for the five-star hotel - that was New York City fantasy too, unless the Commissioner was talking about the sleazy no-tell motel across College Point Boulevard.

When the seminar ended I left the classroom and walked down the long hallway towards the open stairway. Several classrooms lined my path along the wide walkway. A new recruit class had been sworn in a few days earlier and the 4 x 12 shift at the academy was about to begin. I passed a couple of classrooms and could see it really was one of the very first days of training because the recruits were dressed in business attire as opposed to the NYPD recruit uniform. About a hundred feet ahead of me was the stairway, but just before the stairs was one more classroom. A short, sturdy looking Hispanic male in a gray suit stood outside the classroom door. This was obviously the company sergeant on the lookout for an instructor. I was immediately transported back to that day years ago in the basement of the Police Academy on 20th Street when I was approaching the room for my first class as an instructor.

As I drew closer to the company sergeant I heard him warn the class to "stand by."

Wait a minute – he thinks I'm the instructor. For a split second I considered entering the classroom and watching the recruits all spring to attention – I didn't. Instead, I kept walking to the stairs, but as I passed the company sergeant I reached out, put my hand on his shoulder and said, "Have a great career, my friend."

I squinted in the late afternoon sunlight as I walked across the parking lot. I could feel the rubber band break one last time and I knew it would never pull me back to the Police Academy again.

Made in the USA
Columbia, SC
09 March 2021